# MONEYWISE DICTIONARY
# OF PERSONAL FINANCE

The Financial Post
# MONEYWISE
MAGAZINE

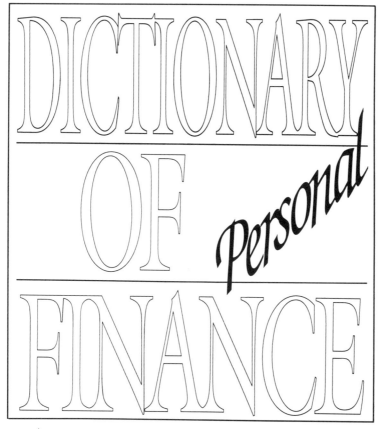

DICTIONARY
OF
*Personal*
FINANCE

## ANDREW WEINER

**Random House**
*Toronto*

Published in Canada in 1987 by Random House of Canada Limited, Toronto.

**Canadian Cataloguing in Publication Data**

Weiner, Andrew.
The Financial Post moneywise magazine book of financial terms

ISBN 0-394-22007-2

I. Finance - Dictionaries. I. Title.

HG151.W44 1987 332'.03'21 C86-094600-2


DESIGN: Brant Cowie/Artplus Ltd.

Printed in Canada

# Contents

*Foreword*

CHAPTER 1
*Personal Budgeting*    *1*

CHAPTER 2
*Real Estate*    *9*

CHAPTER 3
*Financial Services*    *33*

CHAPTER 4
*Life and Health Insurance*    *55*

CHAPTER 5
*Property and Casualty Insurance*    *77*

CHAPTER 6
*Investing in the Markets*    *93*

CHAPTER 7
*Personal Taxation*    *123*

CHAPTER 8
*Retirement*    *155*

CHAPTER 9
*Family Finances and Estate Planning*    *173*

*Index*    *191*

# Foreword

The editors of *The Financial Post Moneywise Magazine* have long been interested in personal money—both as a topic for readers and a nice thing to have in your pocket. For the past three years, we have written about people and money and money and people: who has it, who hasn't, where it comes from, where it goes, how to save it, how to spend it, how to make it, how to make more of it.

It's a subject as closely watched as interest rates—*and* as variable and confusing. That's why, when Random House approached us about doing a book on personal money, we felt that first and foremost it should define the territory. Sure, we replied, we'll do a dictionary.

They loved it.

We liked the idea partly because we like dictionaries (and can happily fritter away a morning in pursuit of the meanings of life), but mostly because we could never find any dictionary devoted solely to personal money. There were books on investing, on finance, on taxation, on retirement, on the stock market, each with their little glossaries, but no one handy straightforward reference that put it all together. So we decided to do a book that would serve us and our readers; we just wish we could have found a shorter title.

We asked Andrew Weiner, a well-known freelancer and regular contributor to *The Financial Post Moneywise Magazine* for the past nine years, to research and write the definitions, drawing from a variety of sources and experts. Then we vetted each chapter with more experts to catch any glitches and to make sure we really did know our debits from our debentures.

Of course, being editorial types, we had to add our own touch in-house. Most closely involved from the magazine were Catherine Collins, then managing editor and now editor, who did the major editing of the book and was largely responsible for the flashes of wit that leaven some of the weightier definitions, and Paul Rush, then editor and now publisher, who lent a critical eye and humorous hand to each stage of the manuscript. The result, we hope, is a personal money dictionary that will both help you come to terms with this ever-more complicated financial world and give you a chuckle or two when you're standing in line at your neighborhood ATM.

THE FINANCIAL POST MONEYWISE MAGAZINE

# Acknowledgements

Several professionals graciously donated their time and expertise to our dictionary, reading and vetting various chapters once, twice, sometimes three times when necessary. The Financial Post Moneywise Magazine would like to thank for their contribution:

Irene Bailey, Irene Bailey Insurance Agency, Toronto, Ont.

Corrado Cardarelli, tax lawyer, and Heather Hisey, estates and trusts lawyer, Tory Tory DesLauriers & Binnington, Toronto, Ont.

David Coates, manager, media relations, SunLife of Canada, Toronto, Ont.

Arthur B.C. Drache, barrister and solicitor, Drache, Rotenburg, Ottawa, Ont.

Christopher Jackson, agent, Mutual Life Assurance Co., Toronto, Ont.

Audrey M. Loeb, barrister and solicitor, Widman & Loeb, Toronto, Ont.

James Micules and Dennis Thacker, chartered accountants, Pannell Kerr MacGillivray Chartered Accountants, Mississauga, Ont.

Carol Street, barrister and solicitor, Bogart Russell Campbell Robertson, Toronto, Ont.

Brenda M. Wilson, senior account executive, Nesbitt Thomson Deacon Inc., Toronto, Ont.

The Society of Fellows of the Insurance Institute of Canada, Toronto, Ont.

# CHAPTER ONE

# *Personal Budgeting*

**asset:**   anything of monetary value owned by an individual or business.

---

**balance sheet:**   a formal statement indicating the
financial condition of an individual or business at a
specific point in time. The balance sheet lists assets in
the left-hand column, liabilities in the right-hand
column and net worth at the bottom. Drawing up such
a balance sheet is a vital, although sobering, component of financial planning, especially if your
leanings are toward the right.

---

**bankruptcy:**   the legal conditions under which a
debtor has been declared bankrupt, or financially in-
solvent, by court proceedings, and whose financial affairs are being administered by the court through a
receiver or trustee. May be applied for voluntarily, or
petitioned for by creditors.

---

**budget:**   a formal estimate of future income and expenses, used for financial planning. For individuals,
the process of budgeting involves establishing a spending plan in line with income estimates. For those
whose spending plans are way out of line, *see* **bankruptcy**.

---

**capital:**   tangible wealth that can be invested to
produce additional wealth. What do you not do with
your capital? You never, never live *on* your capital—although if you invest it wisely, you may live off it.

---

**cash budget:**   a statement of income and expendi-
ture based solely on cash inflows and outflows over a
specified period. What you may need if you find your-

self running to the ATM (automated-teller machine) five times a week.

---

**cash flow:**  the movement of cash into, through and out of a particular entity, whether it be an individual's accounts or those of a business. Into is better than out of.

---

**collectible:**  an item held and sometimes traded for its value as part of a collection of similar objects, such as stamps, toy soldiers or comic books. Often collected as a (not always reliable) inflation hedge. A premature form of the antique, which is usually defined as an item of value more than 100 years old. For example— grandmother's porcelain, grandmother's jewelry, grandmother....

---

**Consumer Price Index (CPI):**  index compiled by Statistics Canada showing cost–of–living changes. The most widely watched indicator of the rate of inflation.

---

**debt:**  *see* **liabilities.**

---

**deflation:**  a sustained reduction in the general price of goods and services. True deflation has not been experienced in North America since the 1930s, although in recent years we have experienced disinflation, a gradual reduction in the rate of inflation. *Compare* **inflation.**

---

**disposable income:**   the income of an individual available for spending, saving or investment. Technically, all income after taxes is regarded as disposable income; in practice, it's what's left over after paying the mortgage and other essentials. No, a Ferrari 328 GTB is not essential.

---

**equity:**   the monetary value of something owned and paid for. (*See also* pp. 18 and 102.)

---

**expenses:**   in accounting terminology, an expense is a cost incurred in doing business. For an individual, an expense is any money paid out for any purpose—a cost incurred in living (although some live better than others). For details about deductible expenses, *see* p. 131.

---

**financial planning:**   the process of assessing your financial situation, framing objectives and making plans to achieve them. A financial planner assists individuals in this process. Providing financial-planning assistance is a booming profession, but also a totally unregulated one. Some financial planners offer advice in exchange for a fee. Other people who call themselves financial planners are actually selling life insurance, mutual funds or other investment instruments in exchange for a commission. Others again are selling outright scams. Caveat emptor.

---

**fixed costs:**   periodic and continuing costs. For an individual, these include rent or mortgage payments, insurance premiums, property taxes and so on: the overhead on being alive. Your VISA statement, on the other hand, is a variable cost, since it will fluctuate from month to month—although not always in the direction you might like.

**income:** total revenue received from all sources, and the subject of powerful fantasies. One of them may be becoming a financial planner.

**inflation:** a rise in the general level of prices, which leads to reduced purchasing power for the same number of dollars. An inflation hedge is an investment expected to increase in value more rapidly than inflation is increasing. Favorite hedges include gold, real estate and collectibles. Not to be confused with, say, a privet hedge, although you should remember that any hedge can be clipped.

**investment:** something you put money into to make more money. For example, this dictionary.

**investment counselor:** a professional who offers advice on investing in securities, as compared to a financial planner (*see* **financial planning**), who normally takes a broader look at a client's finances.

**liabilities:** amounts owed to creditors. Accounting terminology for debt.

**net assets:** *see* **net worth.**

**net income:** total income, less expenses incurred to earn it, before you pay taxes on it. (For Revenue Canada's definition, *see* p. 143.) What you like to think you're worth. And now for something completely different...

---

**net worth:**  the value of your total assets minus your total liabilities. The net worth of an individual includes personal as well as business assets and liabilities. The very bottom line.

---

**opportunity cost:**  the benefits given up by choosing one spending alternative over another. For example, if you use $10,000 to take an exotic vacation, the opportunity cost is the rate of return that money might have earned, or how it might have appreciated, elsewhere—say, in Canada Savings Bonds or stocks or a house.

---

**personal income:**  gross income received by an individual from all non-business sources, including salary and investment income, before taxes are paid.

---

**variable costs:**  costs that change from month to month rather than being predictable and fixed. These are the ones that can get you into trouble. *Compare* **fixed costs.**

---

CHAPTER TWO

# Real
# Estate

**adverse possession:** acquiring actual possession of a property without the owner's consent.

---

**agent:** an individual authorized to transact business on another person's behalf. In real estate, a broker or a salesperson employed by a broker acts as the seller's agent in the sale of a property. By law, a real-estate salesperson is always the seller's agent, never the buyer's. In good times, they all drive moss-green Mercedes.

---

**agreement of purchase and sale:** written agreement between buyer and seller in which the buyer agrees to buy a property and the seller agrees to sell it in accordance with the terms of the agreement. *See* **offer to purchase.**

---

**amortization:** the gradual paying off of a debt by periodic installments. The number of years required to repay the debt in full is called the amortization period, and may be much greater than the loan's term. For example, you might have a mortgage with a five-year term amortized over twenty-five years. An amortization schedule is a table showing the principal and interest payments and the unpaid loan balance for each payment period of the loan. And you thought Dostoevsky was depressing reading.

---

**appraiser:** individual hired to estimate a property's value. Often employed by the lender, at the expense of the buyer, where the property is being offered as security for a mortgage loan. The appraised value for mortgage-lending purposes is typically highly conservative, and may underestimate market value.

---

**appreciation:** increase in the value of property. Your profit margin on selling (less real-estate commission, legal fees and carrying charges).

---

**assessed value:** valuation placed upon your property as a basis for municipal taxation. Typically, you would prefer the assessed value to be low and the appraised value to be high. Your annual assessment is the amount of municipal tax you owe.

---

**assumption of mortgage:** where the buyer of a mortgaged property assumes liability for continued payment of the existing mortgage debt. Requires the consent of the lender.

---

**balance due on closing:** the amount the buyer is required to pay the vendor to complete the purchase after various adjustments (for example, utility payments) are made. *See also* **statement of adjustments.**

---

**balloon payment:** a final payment on your mortgage greater than the preceding installments that repays the loan in full. You would make a balloon payment, for example, on a mortgage loan that required interest-only payments, or payments for small amounts of principal and interest, with the principal due at the end of the loan period. Rare in Canada, common practice in the United States.

---

**blended payments:** payments on a mortgage loan that combine principal and interest.

---

**blended rate:**  an interest rate applied to a refinanced loan that is higher than the rate on the old loan but lower than current new-loan rates. May be applied when a buyer assumes an existing mortgage at lower-than-current rates and asks the lender to increase the size of the loan.

---

**bridging loan:**  financing used to bridge the gap between the purchase of one property and the sale of another when the proceeds of the sale are to be used to offset the purchase.

---

**broker:**  in real estate, an individual licensed under provincial law to act as an agent for property owners in the buying and selling of real estate.

---

**buying down:**  paying the lender to reduce the interest rate on a mortgage loan. In periods of high mortgage rates, a seller may do this in order to offer a more attractive mortgage on a property. At the end of the term, the mortgage is renewed at current rates. Gains here may be illusory: the vendor may add the cost of the "buy down" to the purchase price of the property. More common in the new housing than resale market.

---

**Canada Mortgage and Housing Corporation (CMHC):** a federal Crown corporation. The CMHC provides housing information and assistance to consumers, and insures mortgage loans for lenders.

---

**Canadian Real Estate Association (CREA):**  the national voice of the Canadian real-estate industry. While made up predominantly of real-estate brokers and salespeople, its membership also includes appraisers, property managers and developers.

---

**capital gains tax:**   *see* p. 129.

---

**carrying charges:**   the expenses involved in holding, or "carrying," a property. The term is applied by real-estate developers to describe the expenses, such as interest costs and taxes, involved in holding property or land that is either sitting idle or under construction or renovation. For a homeowner, the term is sometimes applied to cover all outgoings: mortgage, taxes, insurance, utilities and so on. Some carrying charges require more financial muscle than others.

---

**chattel:**   personal property. Anything tangible, other than real estate, such as furniture, an automobile, jewelry.

---

**clear title:**   *see* **title search.**

---

**closed mortgage:**   a mortgage with no provision for prepayment prior to maturity. Prepayment may still be allowed at the discretion of the lender, but usually at a cost of at least three months' interest payments.

---

**closing:**   the act of transferring ownership of property from seller to buyer under the terms of the agreement of purchase and sale. Also used to refer to the closing date. *See also* **closing costs.**

**closing costs:**  the fees and expenses payable by the buyer and seller at the time of closing of a real-estate transaction. For the buyer, these may include legal fees, land transfer tax, inspection and appraisal fees, fees to register the deed and so on. Often under-estimated at time of purchase. (There goes that new living-room sofa.)

---

**closing date:**  the date specified in the agreement of purchase and sale, on which the buyer delivers the balance of the money due and the seller delivers the deed and (unless otherwise agreed) vacant possession of the property.

---

**cloud on title:**   *see* **title search.**

---

**collateral mortgage:**  loan secured by a mortgage on a property. The money may be used for the purchase of that property or for other purposes, such as home renovations or the purchase of investments.

---

**commercial property:**  property designed for use by retail, wholesale, office or service users, rather than for residential purposes.

---

**commission:**  remuneration paid to a real-estate broker on the sale of a property, usually a percentage of the purchase price.

---

**compounding interest:**  mortgage borrowers pay compound interest—that is, interest on the interest owing, as well as interest on the loan itself. How often interest is compounded affects the total amount of in-terest paid on the mortgage: the more frequent the compounding, the more interest you pay. Traditional mortgages are usually compounded semiannually, that is twice a year. However, some mortgages, such as variable-rate mortgages, are compounded monthly. For example, a variable-rate mortgage with a nominal rate of 10% compounded monthly actually has an effective interest rate of 10.47%—and is sure to give you a compounding headache.

---

**conditional offer:**   offer to purchase a property valid only if certain conditions are met. For example, you may offer to buy a home only if you are able to sell your current home, or only if the vendor agrees to take back a mortgage (*see* **vendor take back**). In a strong real-estate market, that is, one where there are more buyers than sellers, vendors will be more prepared to wait for an unconditional offer, with no such conditions attached.

---

**condominium:**   system of ownership of in-dividual units in a multiple-unit building, with joint ownership of commonly used property, and with joint responsibility for paying for maintenance of these common areas.

---

**construction lien:**   *see* **lien.**

---

**conventional mortgage:**   a mortgage loan of no more than seventy-five percent of the appraised value or purchase price of a property, whichever is lower. Mortgages exceeding this ceiling must be insured.

---

**conveyance:** the actual transfer of ownership of a property from one person to another at the closing. Bread and butter for your family lawyer.

---

**cooperative:** system of ownership in which the owner has a share in a cooperative building; the cooperative actually owns the property. This share gives the right to live in a housing unit, but does not give ownership of the unit. Classy in New York City, but usually not-for-profit in Canada.

---

**deed:** a form of document that conveys title or interest in a property.

---

**default:** is your fault. It means failure to repay an outstanding debt as agreed. On a mortgage, may result in foreclosure or power of sale.

---

**deposit:** money paid by the buyer as a pledge to fulfill the agreement to buy, held by the broker or vendor's lawyer in an escrow account until closing.

---

**detached:** house with freestanding external walls. *Compare* **semidetached,** attached to only one other house by a party wall, and **row house,** where three or more houses are attached in a line.

---

**discharge:** to pay off a debt in full. Oh happy day.

---

**down payment:** cash put down by the buyer of a house.

---

**duplex:** two dwelling units under one roof. Also a "Manhattan duplex"—an apartment on two floors.

---

**easement:** a right enjoyed by one party over the land of another, for example, the right of the telephone company to lay lines on your property; the right of way of a neighbor to cross your property to reach the road. Closely related to "appeasement," which is what you'll require if they tiptoe through your tulips.

---

**effective interest rate:** the actual (as opposed to nominal) interest rate on a variable-rate mortgage, reflecting the effect of monthly compounding. *See also* **compounding interest.**

---

**equity:** the homeowner's equity in a property is the difference between the price at which the property could be sold and the total debt outstanding against it.

---

**escrow account:** where a real-estate broker parks the home buyer's deposit until a deal is concluded. Also called a trust account.

---

**exclusive listing:** where a vendor gives a real-estate broker the sole right to offer a property for sale. Usually carries a lower commission than a multiple listing, but the number of potential buyers is also reduced. As a general rule, even where a broker does have an exclusive listing, he or she will usually cooperate with an agent from another broker who brings a potential customer for the property; they usually agree to split the commission (and kiss those moss-green Mercedes goodbye).

---

**first mortgage:**   the mortgage agreement with first claim on the property in the event of default. Usually carries a lower interest rate than more risky second and third mortgages.

---

**fixed-rate mortgage:**   a mortgage loan for which the rate is fixed for a specified term. *Compare* **variable-rate mortgage.**

---

**fixtures:**   improvements or personal property attached to a property that may not be removed when the house is sold. An area of some potential controversy. Buyers and sellers should spell out what constitutes fixtures as part of the agreement of purchase and sale. For example, is the crystal chandelier yours or theirs?

---

**floating-rate mortgage:**   *see* **variable-rate mortgage.**

---

**foreclosure:**   action by mortgagee to gain ownership of a mortgaged property when default occurs on a mortgage.

---

**frontage:**   the width of a lot along a street or body of water.

---

**gentrification:**   rehabilitation of an older declining neighborhood by a new influx of higher-income residents, which displaces former lower-income residents. Also known as "white painting." Buyers at the frontiers of gentrification may see more rapid appreciation in the values of their homes than in better-established

neighborhoods, but must put up with some of the in-
conveniences of frontier life—restive natives, lack of
fresh pasta and so on.

---

**gross debt service ratio (GDS):** the percentage
of gross annual income required to cover payments for
housing, including mortgages, taxes, heating and a
proportion of condominium fees where applicable.
Mortgage lenders typically allow a maximum GDS of
thirty percent.

---

**handyman's special:** it has walls and windows,
or window frames, anyway. What more do you want?

---

**high-ratio mortgage:** a conventional first-
mortgage loan, but in excess of seventy-five percent
of the appraised value or purchase price of the
property. Must be insured.

---

**holdback:** money not paid until all contractual
commitments are met. For example, a portion of the
value of a renovation contract that is held back until all
work is completed to the homeowner's satisfaction.

---

**homeowner's policy:** insurance policy providing package protection against fire, theft, personal
liability and so on. Where a mortgage is registered on
a property, fire coverage must be at least equal to the
amount of the mortgage.

---

**income property:** real estate that generates income, for example an apartment building or an office
building. Also known as an investment property. Bad

tenants, unexpected expenses or a declining real-estate market may turn it into a divestment property.

---

**interest:** amount charged by lenders for the use of their money.

---

**interest adjustment date (IAD):** date when interest on money advanced before that time is calculated and must be paid by the borrower. When you purchase a home, the interest adjustment date is usually set one month before regular mortgage payments begin.

---

**joint tenancy:** ownership of property by two or more persons. If one dies, the survivor or survivors take exclusive ownership. *Contrast* **tenancy in common.**

---

**land transfer tax:** tax payable by the purchaser of a property; approximately one percent of the purchase price.

---

**lease:** a contract for the right to exclusively use a particular piece of property for a specified period of time in exchange for the payment of rent. The lease spells out the rights and duties of the landlord and the tenant (a good thing since they are rarely on speaking terms). If you rent out a property, make sure you have your tenant sign one. Then if things don't work out, at least the lease, if not your tenant, will expire.

---

**leasehold mortgage:** a mortgage loan used to purchase a building on rented land.

---

**lease with option to purchase:** a rental agreement giving the tenant the right to purchase the leased property at an agreed price under agreed-upon conditions.

---

**legal fees:** expenses incurred in closing on a house, for services including title search and registration of mortgages. The buyer is also responsible for the lender's legal costs, although in many cases the lender will allow the buyer's lawyer to act for both parties. Legal fees are usually set as a percentage of the purchase price. Colloquially known as "legals."

---

**lessee:** tenant under a lease.

---

**lessor:** landlord.

---

**leverage:** making maximum use of borrowed funds for an investment, with the intention of maximizing its profitability. In real estate, buying an expensive house with a small down payment is a form of leverage, since an expensive house that increases in value by ten percent will be more profitable, when sold, than a less expensive house whose value increases at the same rate. As in any form of investment, reverse, or negative, leverage remains a possibility. For example, in a declining real-estate market, the expensive house may lose more in value than the less expensive house, increasing your loss—and decreasing your lever fever.

---

**liability insurance:** protection for the property owner against claims arising from injuries or damages to other people or their property.

---

**lien:** a charge against property, which makes that property security for the payment of a debt. For example, if the owner of a house does not pay a contractor for renovation work, the contractor may file for a construction lien against the property. If the owner then attempts to sell the property, this registered encumbrance will be revealed in the title search. Nobody likes to be liened on.

---

**listing:** agreement between a property owner and a real-estate broker authorizing the broker to offer the property for sale or lease. May be exclusive or multiple. The broker or salesperson who signs up the customer and gets his or her name on the for-sale sign is called the listing agent.

---

**loan-to-value ratio:** the amount of a mortgage loan, expressed as a percentage of the appraised value or purchase price of the property, whichever is less.

---

**market price:** the actual price paid in a real-estate transaction. May be more or less than the market value, a theoretical price estimate. For example, an appraisal may indicate that, in a normally active market, a house should sell for $100,000 within a reasonable period of time. A seller in a great hurry, however, might accept less; a buyer with more money than sense may offer more.

---

**maturity date:** the last day of the term of a mortgage agreement, at which time the mortgage must either be renewed or paid in full. The day of reckoning.

---

**MLS:**   *see* **multiple listing.**

---

**mortgage:**   a long-term recorded note securing the debt that provides cash with which to buy property. The property itself is always in the name of the mortgagor rather than the lender, but serves as the lender's security in case of default in repayment of the debt.

---

**mortgage broker:**   individual who places loans with investors in exchange for a fee. The broker does not service these loans. Source of second-mortgage financing when conventional sources run dry. Brokers also resell vendor-take-back mortgages.

---

**mortgage insurance:**   term usually applied to a life-insurance policy guaranteeing repayment of a mortgage loan in the event of death (or in some cases disability) of the mortgagor. Also applied to insurance for the lender in the event of default, such as the coverage provided by the CMHC.

---

**mortgagee:**   the lender or creditor who accepts a property as security for a debt.

---

**mortgage commitment:**   formal commitment by a lender to grant a mortgage loan for a specified amount under specified conditions.

---

**mortgage loan:**   loan in which some form of property is the security.

---

**mortgagor:**   the borrower, who puts up his or her property as security in exchange for a loan.

---

**multiple listing:**   agreement among brokers to provide information about their listings to each other, to look at offers on their own listings made through other brokers and to split the commission if a sale should result. When brokers talk about "putting a house on MLS," they are referring to the multiple-listing service provided by their local real-estate board.

---

**nominal rate:**   the quoted interest rate for a mortgage loan. The effective interest rate may be higher, depending on the terms of the loan. *See* **compounding interest.**

---

**offer to purchase:**   formal offer to buy a property, presented in the form of an agreement of purchase and sale. May be conditional or unconditional. If the specified price or conditions are unacceptable to the vendor (also known as making an offer he or she *can* refuse), they may be either rejected or signed back at a higher price or with different conditions ("hands off the crystal chandelier"). Once signed by both parties, the offer becomes a legally binding contract.

---

**open house:**   opening a home for sale for inspection by real-estate agents, prospective buyers and neighborhood snoops. ("I always knew they had terrible taste, Fred, but flocked velvet wallpaper?!")

---

**open listing:**   listing given to a number of brokers, any one of whom may sell the property.

---

**open mortgage:**   mortgage agreement allowing the borrower to repay part or all of the debt earlier than specified, usually without prepayment charges.

---

**option:**   the right to purchase (or lease) a property under specified terms within a specified period.

---

**overimprove:**   to spend more on upgrading a property than will be reflected in its final market value, usually by making improvements that would not be appreciated by the average buyer in that neighborhood. And we're not talking flocked velvet wallpaper.

---

**personal use property:**   *see* p. 186.

---

**PIT:**   principal, interest and taxes. Some mortgage agreements ask the borrower to contribute to an escrow account, set up by the lender, to pay property taxes on the mortgaged property. However, principal-and-interest-only mortgage agreements are now more common.

---

**possession:**   the holding, control or custody of property for one's own use.

---

**power of sale:**   the right of a lender to force the sale of a property in the event of default on the terms of the mortgage. Bargains may sometimes be acquired in this way.

---

**prepayment clause:** mortgage clause giving the mortgagor the right to pay a portion of the mortgage debt before it is due.

---

**principal:** the amount borrowed. Also, the client of a real-estate broker.

---

**principal residence:** the place you live in most of the time. Important for tax purposes, since no capital gains tax (*see* p. 129) is payable on the sale of a taxpayer's principal residence.

---

**property tax:** municipal levy based on the assessed value of a property.

---

**raw material:** extreme form of a handyman's special. Almost unlivable, but may be reshaped into your dream home—albeit at nightmarish expense.

---

**real property:** lands and buildings, and objects attached thereto (for example, built-in oven, built-in shelves).

---

**realtor:** real-estate professional belonging to a real-estate board affiliated with the Canadian Real Estate Association.

---

**refinance:** to pay off an existing mortgage and arrange another with the same or another lender.

---

**registered encumbrance:** legal claim against property, including liens and debts for which it has been pledged as security. Obstacle to the transfer of clear title to a property.

---

**RHOSP:** Registered Home Ownership Savings Plan. Tax-exempt savings for the purchase of a principal residence. Sadly, the federal government withdrew its RHOSPitality in 1985.

---

**replacement cost:** the cost of replacing a structure that has been destroyed. Homeowner's insurance should reflect the replacement cost of the building rather than the market value (*see* p. 109) of the building plus land.

---

**right of way:** the right to pass over another person's land for access purposes. A form of easement. A public right of way is an area of a subdivision dedicated to use for roads, streets and other public access.

---

**second mortgage:** a mortgage loan granted when there is already one mortgage registered against the property. In the event of default, the first mortgage is paid before the second from the proceeds of the sale of the property. Typically carries a higher interest rate to reflect the higher risk.

---

**security:** property offered as collateral for a loan.

---

**semidetached:** house attached to another on one side only. The common wall is known as the party wall because when they party, they had better invite you.

---

**sign back:** when presented with an offer to purchase, a vendor may make certain changes before returning it, or "signing it back," to the prospective buyer as part of a process of negotiation. For example, a house is listed for $250,000, but the buyer offers $200,000. The vendor signs it back at $230,000. If the buyer accepts that price, the agreement becomes binding. Sign backs are the reason agents stay up late at night—driving to and from vendors and buyers in their moss-green Mercedes.

---

**speculator:** one who invests in real estate with the expectation of rapid resale (or "flipping") of the property at a higher price.

---

**statement of adjustments:** statement prepared by a lawyer (or a notary in Quebec) setting out the credits to the vendor (such as purchase price, prepaid taxes and insurance) and to the purchaser (such as deposits and tax arrears) and the balance due on closing.

---

**take back:** *see* **vendor take back.**

---

**tax lien:** debt attached against a property for failure to pay taxes. *See also* **lien.**

---

**tenancy in common:** ownership of property by two or more persons in which each person's share will pass to his or her estate in the event of death. *Contrast* **joint tenancy**, where the deceased person's interest passes to the surviving co-owners.

---

**term:**   in a mortgage agreement, the period of time for which the interest rate is fixed. One always wants to be in on good terms.

---

**time is of the essence clause:**   requirement for punctual performance of a contract on the closing date in an agreement of purchase and sale.

---

**title:**   documentary evidence of ownership.

---

**title search:**   examination of the public records to determine the ownership of a property and to find out if there are any clouds on it, such as an outstanding claim or registered encumbrance, that would impair the vendor's title. In the absence of such clouds, the vendor can deliver clear title to the property—a critical requirement not only for the buyer but also for the mortgage lender. The title search should always be carried out by the buyer's lawyer.

---

**total debt service ratio (TDS):**   the percentage of gross annual income required to cover payments associated with housing and all other debts and obligations, such as credit-card balances and car-loan payments.

---

**townhouse:**   home with two or more floors, attached to other similar units via party walls. (A row house by any other name....)

---

**trust account:**   *see* **escrow account.**

---

**unconditional offer:**  offer to buy a property at a specified price with no conditions attached. Once accepted by the vendor, the offer becomes binding. Also known as a firm offer, or "Oh-my-God-what-have-I-done?" *Compare* **conditional offer.**

---

**valuation:**  *see* **appraisal.**

---

**variable-rate mortgage:** mortgage loan for which the rate of interest changes as market conditions change. Monthly payments usually remain stable as interest rates go up, but more of the payment is applied to the interest and less to the principal. If interest rates go up a great deal, the amount of principal owing may actually increase. Also called a floating-rate mortgage.

---

**vendor take back:**  agreement by the seller of a property to provide ("take back") a mortgage to the buyer to facilitate the sale. In periods of high mortgage rates, the vendor may take back a first mortgage at a lower-than-going interest rate. Or a vendor may take back a second mortgage on the property, if the buyer obtains a conventional mortgage for seventy-five percent of the assessed value but still cannot meet the purchase price.

---

**wraparound mortgage:**  the combination of an existing mortgage, usually at a lower-than-going interest rate, with an additional mortgage, usually at a higher rate. Both mortgages are then treated as a single loan.

---

**zoning:**  specifications for the permitted uses of land and size of building in particular areas under local bylaws. A neighborhood's zoning may, for example, permit only single-family residential homes, or it may allow multi-unit dwellings, commercial uses and so on. You might like to check the zoning bylaws before you buy: if a meat-packing plant moves in next door, your home sweet home may turn sour.

———————————————

CHAPTER THREE

# Financial Services

**assets:**  something you own of monetary value. Potential collateral for a loan.

---

**ATM:**  automated-teller machine. Using a bank card and your PIN (personal identification number), you can withdraw cash, make deposits, transfer money between accounts, pay bills and perform other routine transactions without setting foot in a bank. Progress in action—rather than having to queue up inside your local bank, you can queue up outside it instead.

---

**bank:**  in Canada, a federally chartered financial organization with powers defined under the Bank Act. Despite a progressive blurring of boundaries between the banks and other financial institutions, such as trust companies, banks retain dominance in commercial lending. Banks are restricted from entering areas such as fiduciary services, although legislation is pending that may allow them to enter the securities field. (*See also* **four pillars**.) Banks fall into one of two categories; *see* **Schedule A bank**.

---

**Bank Act:**  Canadian federal legislation governing the operations of banks. Revised every ten years.

---

**bank card:**  term applied to plastic credit cards issued by banks (VISA and Mastercard), although the same cards are also issued by some trust companies. Non-bank credit cards for travel and entertainment, such as American Express and Diners Club, and cards issued by retailers or oil companies on charge accounts, are sometimes referred to as "charge cards."

---

36                                          FINANCIAL SERVICES

**bank draft:** a check made out to a specific individual or company drawn by a bank on its own funds on deposit with another bank. For example, a bank draft purchased at a Canadian bank may be sent to an individual in the United States and cashed there by a correspondent bank of the domestic bank that issued the draft.

---

**bank failure:** temporary or permanent closure of a bank due to failure to meet the withdrawal demands of its depositors. Remember the 1985 collapse of the Canadian Commercial Bank? In some cases, failure may be disguised by merger with a stronger bank. In Canada, depositors' funds are only partly insured by the Canada Deposit Insurance Corporation in the event of bank failure. As safe as money in the bank, you say?

---

**bank money order:** a money instrument purchased from a bank for its face amount plus a small fee, and sent to its payee for conversion into cash. Typically used by those without checking accounts as a means of sending money by mail. Banks also sell international money orders, which are negotiable in a variety of foreign currencies.

---

**bank statement:** statement of a depositor's account, usually sent out monthly. But don't shoot the messenger.

---

**Canada Deposit Insurance Corporation (CDIC):** government body that provides insurance for deposits in banks and trust companies, to a maximum of $60,000 per depositor in each institution. Individuals are also insured for any RRSP (*see* p. 167) holdings in the form of deposits, to a maximum of an additional

$60,000 in each institution. Deposits with financial institutions incorporated in the province of Quebec get separate but equal protection under the Quebec Deposit Insurance Act. Deposits cover the range from checking and savings account balances to term deposits and GICs. Note, however, that there is *no* insurance on term deposits and GICs with a duration longer than five years.

**Canada Savings Bond** (CSB): federal government bond, issued each year on November 1, carrying a rate of interest fixed for a year or more. Among the safest, most liquid and—the government would like you to think—most patriotic of all investment vehicles.

**cashier's check:** a bank's check, signed by an officer of the bank, issued for several purposes, including deposit transfers, bill payments and loans.

**cashless society:** the banker's vision of Utopia— a world in which paper money and checks have been entirely replaced by the use of credit cards and debit cards, which allow payment for any goods and services through electronic funds transfer. The poker game just won't be the same.

**certificate of deposit:** negotiable money-market instrument issued by banks in large denominations. Also, nonnegotiable receipt for a bank deposit, for example a term deposit, in certificate rather than passbook form, stating the amount of the deposit, rate of interest and repayment terms.

**certified check:** a check drawn on a bank depositor's account and guaranteed by the bank on which it is drawn. After setting aside enough of the depositor's funds to cover the check, the bank stamps the face of the check to indicate that it has been certified.

---

**charge card:** non-bank credit card. *See* **bank card, credit card.**

---

**charge account:** credit account offered by a retailer, with specified payment and interest requirements. If you're born to shop, it'll be the death of you.

---

**chartered bank:** bank chartered by the federal government to carry out banking operations in Canada. Formerly a synonym for "Canadian bank," because foreign banks were not allowed to set up and carry out such operations here. Since the 1980 Bank Act permitted foreign banks to operate Schedule B banks (*see* pp. 50–51) in Canada, however, the term has become less meaningful. All banks operating under the Bank Act are now, by definition, chartered banks.

---

**chattel:** any personal property other than real estate. A loan against such property—for example, your car, your Renoir or your stamp collection—is known as a chattel mortgage.

---

**check:** a draft or order drawn on funds on deposit with a bank or other financial institution, payable on demand—although payment may be delayed until the check has cleared.

---

**checking account:** an account holding credit balances against which a depositor may draw checks. In a pure checking account, the bank pays no interest on the funds deposited. However, the traditional distinction between checking accounts and savings accounts has eroded in recent years, with the advent of hybrid products such as checking/savings accounts, on which the consumer can write checks *and* earn interest. Doing both can be a tricky balancing act.

---

**clearing:** the process through which a bank collects payment for checks drawn on other banks and makes payment for those drawn on its own depositors' accounts.

---

**collateral:** the security pledged to ensure repayment of a loan. You see, it's not whether you've got what it takes, but whether they'll take what you've got.

---

**compound interest:** the "interest on interest"— the interest earned on a principal sum of money being added to that principal for purposes of calculating future interest. Better to receive than to give. *Compare* **simple interest.**

---

**consumer loan:** loan obtained from a financial institution by an individual rather than a commercial borrower for personal expenditures, such as automobiles, home improvements and so on.

---

**correspondent bank:**   foreign bank maintaining a formal relationship with a Canadian bank, or vice versa; for example, for international transfer of funds via a bank draft.

---

**co-sign:**   when an individual fails to qualify for a loan on his or her own account, the lender may permit a responsible guarantor to co-sign it, thereby assuming joint and several responsibility for repayment. In guarantor they trust.

---

**counter check:**   a blank check made available by a bank or retailer for the convenience of depositors who do not have their own checks with them. Gradually becoming unavailable because of the computerization of banking and because of personalized checks.

---

**credit bureau:**   clearing house for credit-history information used by lenders in assessing consumer-loan applications. Information is provided by member institutions including banks, trust companies, retailers and other lenders and gathered from public records, such as bankruptcy proceedings. It pays to check your file for errors: mis-history repeats itself.

---

**credit card:**   plastic card issued by financial institution or retailer allowing purchase of goods or services up to a predetermined credit limit. Some cards, such as American Express, require immediate settlement of the account on receipt of the statement. Others, such as VISA and Mastercard, in effect provide a permanent line of credit, as long as regular interest payments are made. However, the interest rate is much higher than for regular consumer loans. Most financial institutions also charge either an annual or per-transaction fee for the use of their cards. A good way to buy; a bad way to borrow. *See also* **bank card, charge card.**

---

**credit rating:** assessment of credit-worthiness, based largely on previous behavior in repaying debts as revealed by information provided by the applicant and in some cases also obtained from a credit bureau. No news is usually good news.

---

**credit union:** a nonprofit cooperative financial institution, designed to encourage savings by its members and to make loans to them, usually regulated by provincial statute.

---

**daily-interest checking account** (DICA): form of checking/savings account in which interest, calculated daily, is paid on funds kept on deposit. Typically, interest is paid only when the depositor maintains a certain level of funds, and is lower than that paid on a daily-interest savings account.

---

**daily-interest savings account** (DISA): passbook savings account on which interest is calculated on each day's balance. Compare a traditional passbook savings account, on which interest is paid at a higher rate but is based on the smallest balance on deposit that month. Now you, too, can be a teller.

---

**debit:** any charge on an account. ("We have today debited your checking account....") A debit a day keeps the creditor away.

---

**debit card:**  instrument of payment authorizing the bank to debit your account for a purchase on receipt of details of the transaction from the retailer. *Compare* **credit card,** where the bank or other institution provides credit until the eventual settlement of the debt. Debit cards already exist, on an experimental basis, but their widespread use awaits the advent of electronic funds transfer, which would permit instantaneous debiting. *See also* **preauthorized payments**, in which debits are made without a debit card.

**debt load:**  the sum of debt you are currently carrying. Debt service is the amount you must pay to carry that load. The bigger they are, the harder you crawl.

**demand deposit:**  a deposit with a financial institution that can be claimed by the depositor without advance notice or penalty; for example, your savings-account balance (although there are some high-yielding savings accounts that do require advance notice).

**demand loan:**  a loan with no fixed date of termination, which may be terminated at any time by the lender or borrower, usually carrying a variable interest rate. *Compare* **installment loan.**

**deposit insurance:**  *see* **Canada Deposit Insurance Corporation.**

**direct deposit:**  payment to an individual's account without use of cash or check. The reverse of a preauthorized payment. Many companies arrange the direct deposit of salaries, perhaps in the hope that you won't burn it as soon as you earn it.

**electronic funds transfer** (EFT): electronic rather than paper-based completion of financial transactions, permitting instantaneous movement of money—faster than a speeding Brinks truck. Already widely used in business banking, and soon to become a force in consumer transactions at the retail level. *See also* **debit card.**

---

**endorse:** to sign a document, such as a check, to permit passage of title to that document to another individual or to a financial institution.

---

**escrow:** the money, stocks, deeds or other instruments that are held by a third party until the conditions of a contract between the first and second parties have been met.

---

**fiduciary:** a person or institution holding a relationship of trust in a financial capacity while acting for another; for example, as the executor or administrator of an estate. *See also* **trust company, trustee.**

---

**foreign exchange:** the process of buying or selling foreign currencies, primarily for the settling of international trade transactions. More "Big Bang" for your buck.

---

**four pillars:** traditionally, Canadian regulators have attempted to maintain clear distinction between the "four pillars" of the financial-services industry, each with their unique "core" function: banks (commercial lending), trust companies (fiduciary services), life-insurance companies (insurance underwriting) and brokerage houses (domestic-securities underwriting). While these core differences remain in force, fierce competition for the consumer's business has caused other distinctions to become so blurred that the four pillars are now said to be crumbling. Watch out for falling rates.

---

**frozen account:** it would be nice if this meant cold, hard cash, but in fact it's a bank account on which all transactions have been suspended, by court or government order, to prevent the withdrawal of funds.

---

**garnishment:** court order allowing a creditor to seize, or garnishee, a portion of wages, salaries or bank accounts to obtain repayment of a debt. You might call this a form of capital garnishment, if you find yourself on debt row.

---

**Guaranteed Investment Certificate (GIC):** a certificate of deposit usually issued by a trust company. Very similar to term deposits in a bank, and directly competitive with them. Like a term deposit, a GIC pays a fixed rate of interest over a specified period of time. Interest rates and minimum deposit required vary depending on the institution.

---

**guarantor:** one who co-signs a loan, assuming joint and several responsibility for repayment of the debt. A good way to lose friends.

---

**Inspector General of Banks:** federal-government employee responsible for the administration of the Bank Act, and charged with regularly examining the financial soundness of Canadian banks. Lately, the inspector has been busy.

---

**installment loan:** loan advanced against a promise of regular fixed payments of principal and interest for an agreed term. *Compare* **demand loan.**

---

**Interac:** Canadian network of ATMs, including all major financial institutions, which allows a customer of one financial institution to make a cash withdrawal from the ATM of another institution.

---

**IOU:** a written and signed statement acknowledging a specific amount of debt to another person. It is generally legally enforceable, although it is a non-negotiable debt instrument. Stands for "I owe you," the second three most overused words in the English language.

---

**joint account:** a bank account held in common by two or more parties. Also a good way to lose friends.

---

**joint and several responsibility:** legally, a situation where a lender can demand full repayment from any and all of those who have borrowed. Each borrower is liable for the full debt, not just a prorated share, should one of the other borrowers be unable to meet his or her obligation. Joint and several responsibility also applies when you agree to act as guarantor for someone else's loan.

---

**kiting:**  fraud involving the depositing of a series of checks in a cycle to different banks, each deposit "covering" a previous check that would otherwise bounce, for progressively higher amounts. The practice is rapidly becoming impossible because of instantaneous electronic communications between banks.

---

**leasing:**  buying the right to use a particular item, such as a car, for a specified length of time. An alternative to buying, or more likely, borrowing to buy, that item.

---

**line of credit:**  the maximum amount a customer may borrow, by prearrangement, from a financial institution. Basically an overdraft privilege, allowing the customer to borrow funds without treating each loan as a new one requiring separate approval. The actual amount borrowed may wax and wane as money is paid in and then borrowed again—hence the term "revolving credit." Also called a "credit line." More like a firing line, for those who continually face it.

---

**loan:**  money owned by one party and used by another by mutual consent, to be repaid under specified terms and carrying specified rates of interest.

---

**loan shark:**  an illegal lender, charging excessive rates of interest (even higher than VISA) and typically using unpleasant but effective collection practices. Loan sharks may speak softly, but they carry a big stick. Usually a baseball bat.

---

**MICR:** magnetic-ink character recognition. The markings on a check that allow it to be processed by computer.

---

**multibranch banking:** service permitting bank customers to make transactions at any branch of the same bank anywhere in Canada.

---

**NSF:** cheque returned because there are Not Sufficient Funds. The kiss of debt.

---

**numbered account:** bank account designated by number rather than by name to protect the account owner's anonymity, available in Switzerland and several other countries. Although they evoke cloak-and-dagger images of tax evasion and laundered money, numbered accounts are also legitimate shelters for the rich but honest person's income.

---

**overdraft:** the amount by which a bank has paid checks in excess of the balance in an individual's account.

---

**overdraft protection:** service offered by many banks through which, by prior arrangement, the bank will cover NSF checks up to a certain limit, for a specified minimum charge. *See also* **line of credit.**

---

**overdrawn:** an account is overdrawn when you take out more money than the account actually contains. This is what you might call wishful banking. Banks will no longer permit this to happen without some prior arrangement for overdraft protection.

---

**passbook:**   record-keeping book issued by a bank to its savings depositors in which deposits, withdrawals and interest payments are recorded. Also used in some checking/savings accounts.

---

**pawnbroker:**   one who lends money against personal property at high interest rates. The poor person's banker. Also a good source if you want to buy a used watch or inexpensive engagement ring.

---

**payee:**   the person or organization to which a money instrument, such as a check or money order, is made payable.

---

**payor:**   one who makes a payment.

---

**personal check:**   a check drawn by an individual upon a checking account in that individual's name.

---

**Personal Identification Number** (PIN):   Numerical password issued by financial institutions to users of their ATMs. And don't you forget it.

---

**personal loan:**   loan made to an individual by a lending institution, with or without collateral, including both consumer loans and lines of credit.

---

**POS:**   point of sale. Where you spend your money. Bankers talk a lot about "EFT/POS"; what they're dreaming of is the day, not too far off, when facilities for electronic funds transfer will be installed in retail stores, allowing direct debiting of your bank account for your purchases via a debit card.

**postdated check:**  check dated later than the date on which it is written. Banks cannot cash post-dated checks until they become due.

**preauthorized payment:** money regularly drawn from an individual's bank account by prior arrangement to cover payments for such things as mortgages and insurance policies. The arrangement by which such payments are made is sometimes called a standing order.

**prime lending rate:** the interest rate major banks charge their most creditworthy corporate customers on short-term loans. Used as a guide for setting other interest rates, and for forecasting economic trends. A loan at "prime plus one," for example, carries an interest rate one percent above the current prime lending rate. Prime indicator of how *you* rate.

**promissory note:**  written promise to pay another person a specified sum, at some time in the future or on demand. Similar to an IOU, except that a promissory note is a negotiable instrument that the lender can sell or assign to another party. (*See also* p. 145.)

**reconciliation:** the process of comparing two related records, such as your own record of checking-account transactions and the statement supplied by your bank, and explaining any differences between them. Gross discrepancies may call for rationalization.

**red ink:** a minus entry in accounting records was traditionally written in red ink. Now used generally to refer to losses on an investment. "In the red" is somewhere you don't want to be.

---

**retail banking:** banking services directed at the individual—as opposed to commercial banking, which is directed at business customers.

---

**revolving credit:** debt built up under a line of credit or credit-card balance, which fluctuates in size as funds are paid back and then borrowed again. The lender may let you keep on revolving forever, as long as certain minimum payment requirements are met—or until you're all spun out.

---

**safe-deposit box:** a personal storage box in a vault in a bank where valuables and darkest secrets are kept. Where would the murder mystery be without it?

---

**savings account:** a bank account devoted to the accumulation of savings, which pays interest on the money held in it. Traditionally in sharp contrast to a checking account, which was used for transactions rather than savings, and which carried no interest. Today, however, many accounts offer both savings and checking features. Check them out carefully.

---

**Schedule A bank:** term now used to describe Canadian banks that were in existence prior to the 1980 Bank Act, to distinguish them from the newly created Schedule B banks. The Schedule B category was developed to permit foreign banks to operate in

Canada. One major difference between the two types of banks is in their stock ownership. Shares of Schedule A banks are widely held, with no one interest allowed to hold more than 10%. Shares of Schedule B banks, however, may be more closely held—up to 100% by a single interest. At the same time, Schedule B banks operate under certain restrictions as to their size and number of branches. Typically, the B banks have focused on commercial lending, although a few have moved into the domain of the A banks: retailing banking. Plans were recently abandoned to create a new type of Schedule C bank, which would be able to operate under common ownership with trust and life-insurance companies to create "one-stop shopping" for the consumer of financial services. Remember the days when banking was as simple as ABC?

**secured loan:** a loan secured by collateral or mortgages that can be liquidated to ensure repayment in the event of default.

**service charge:** fee charged by a bank or trust company for a particular service, such as return of canceled checks, transfer of funds between accounts and so on. Just one of the many little ways they bank on you.

**simple interest:** the interest earned on a principal sum of money.

**SMART card:** plastic card with built-in microprocessor-based "memory" to record account balances and transactions, likely to be used in the future with credit cards and debit cards. Already being used as a security check in electronic business banking.

**standing order:**   *see* **preauthorized payment.**

---

**stop payment:**   instruction to a bank from a depositor to withhold payment on a check drawn on the depositor's account. What you probably won't be able to do with a debit card.

---

**SWIFT:**   Society for Worldwide Interbank Financial Telecommunications. Organization for transfer of funds and information among banks around the world.

---

**term deposit:**   a deposit in a bank for a specified period of time at a specified rate of interest, with penalties for early withdrawal. Trust companies, although they may not accept term deposits, issue the very similar GICs. *Compare* **demand deposit.**

---

**three Cs of credit:**   rule of thumb used by lenders in assessing credit worthiness. The three Cs are character (are you prepared to suffer?), capacity (can you make as much as you spend?) and collateral (do you have the right stuff to secure the loan?).

---

**traveler's check:**   negotiable money instrument, available in a variety of foreign currencies and at the rate of exchange on the date of purchase, that you may buy in advance of a trip or extended stay in a foreign country. Notorious for hanging around uncashed for months or years—a kind of interest-free loan from you to the financial institution that issued the check.

---

**Treasury bill:** short-term Government of Canada obligation, bearing no interest but sold at a discount from face value (*see* p. 103). The discount provides the return to T-bill investors.

---

**trust:** a bequest or other device that puts legal title and control of property in the hands of one party, the trustee, for the benefit of another. (*See also* p. 188.)

---

**trust company:** a type of financial institution, either provincially or federally regulated, empowered to handle trusts, either as trustee or as agent for trustees. These fiduciary powers are the so-called "core function" of Canada's trust companies (*see* **four pillars**), not available from other financial institutions. However, trust companies also accept deposits, offer checking accounts, savings vehicles such as GICs and consumer loans, and in other ways function much like banks.

---

**trustee:** individual holding property in trust, charged with ensuring that the proper distribution of income and capital is made.

---

**trustee in bankruptcy:** person appointed to manage the affairs and debts of one who has been declared bankrupt.

---

**trust officer:** person working in the trust and estate-planning functions of a trust company.

---

**variable interest rate:** interest rate on a loan that fluctuates with changes in the prime lending rate.

Common practice in demand loans and some
mortgages.

---

**VCAN:**  Visa Canada Authorization Network. System
developed by the major banks for checking credit-card
purchases at the point of sale, via the retailer's
authorization terminal.

---

# CHAPTER FOUR

# Life and Health Insurance

**accelerated option:** a provision in a life-insurance policy allowing the holder to use the policy's cash value and accumulated dividends to pay up the policy sooner than normal.

**accidental death benefit:** paid when death is caused by accidental bodily injury. Insurance people call it a double-indemnity benefit if attached to a life-insurance policy for the same face amount; Hitchcock fans call it suspicious (*see* **double indemnity**).

**accident and sickness insurance:** form of insurance against expenses or loss of income resulting from accidental injury, illness or accidental death.

**actuary:** a specialist trained in probabilities and statistics who computes statistical tables relating to insurance, and premiums to be charged. Somebody's gotta do it. (*See also* p. 157.)

**agent:** sales and service representative of an insurance company, also called a life underwriter. In life insurance, usually represents one company exclusively. Earns a commission on each policy sold. Rarely the hit of the party, though he or she may find hits *at* the party.

**ancillary benefits:** benefits for miscellaneous hospital and medical charges.

**annual renewable term:** form of term insurance that can be renewed annually without new evidence of insurability; premiums increase annually.

**annuitant:**  individual during whose life an annuity is payable—usually, but not invariably, the person receiving that annuity income.

---

**annuity:**  contract providing income payments at regular (usually monthly) intervals for a specified period. A life annuity provides payments during the lifetime of the annuitant. An annuity certain provides periodic payments over a specified number of years and is not dependent on any person's survival. An annuity consideration is the payment, or series of payments, made to purchase an annuity. *See also* **group annuity, installment refund annuity, joint and last survivor annuity.**

---

**assignment:**  transfer by the owner of an interest in a policy to someone else, either as collateral for a debt or in an actual sale.

---

**automatic-premium loan:**  provision in a participating policy, which allows the insurance company to automatically pay any premium that has not been paid at the end of the grace period with a loan against the existing cash value in the policy.

---

**beneficiary:**  person entitled to collect the insurance money on the death of the insured individual. *See also* **irrevocable beneficiary, contingent beneficiary, primary beneficiary.** The reaper, however grim.

---

**benefit:**  the amount paid under an insurance contract.

---

**benefit period:** time limit on payments under an insurance contract covering, for example, accident, illness or hospital stay. Get well soon.

---

**cash value:** the value of a whole-life or endowment insurance policy the holder would collect if he or she voluntarily canceled the policy before it became payable; also known as the cash surrender value. Life-insurance policies providing a cash surrender value are sometimes called cash-value life insurance. The policyholder may also borrow against this cash value; the rate of interest may or may not be specified in the policy.

---

**certificate of insurance:** document given to a person covered under a group policy, stating the period for which he or she is insured and the nature of the coverage.

---

**Chartered Life Underwriter** (CLU): professional designation for agents who have completed the five-year training course of the Institute of Chartered Life Underwriters of Canada. Ever met an agent who didn't have a CLU?

---

**common disaster:** in life insurance, the simultaneous death of both the insured and the beneficiary (for example, in a car accident). A common-disaster clause in a life-insurance policy provides for proceeds to go to an alternative or contingent beneficiary.

---

**contingent beneficiary:** individual entitled to benefit only after the death of the original or primary beneficiary.

---

**convertible policy:** a term insurance policy that may be exchanged for a whole-life insurance policy without providing evidence of insurability. Also known as convertible term.

---

**coverage:** the amount of protection offered by an insurance policy. Don't get caught in an undercoverage operation.

---

**creditor's group insurance:** life insurance issued on the lives of customers of banks and of other institutional lenders, naming the institution as the beneficiary; if the customer dies, the insurance pays his or her debt.

---

**crisscross insurance:** form of life insurance in which two or more persons insure each others' lives, often used in conjunction with buy-sell agreements (*see* p. 176). Also known as partnership insurance. Or survival of the fittest.

---

**decreasing term insurance:** form of term insurance in which the premiums remain constant while the amount payable slowly decreases in scheduled steps. Bought mostly for mortgage protection.

---

**deferred annuity:** an annuity providing for regular payments to commence at a future date. The question is, can you last from here to annuity?

---

**disability:** inability to work or function on the job or in private life as a result of accident or illness. May be partial or total, temporary or permanent. Disability income insurance provides specific regular payments to an individual who has become disabled. A disability waiver or waiver of premium on a life-insurance policy provides that the insurance company will pay the premium if the policyholder is sick or disabled.

---

**dismemberment benefit:** payable for loss by accident of arms, legs, hands, feet or eyesight. (Are you sure you've got the stomach for this?) Depending on the nature of the dismemberment, payment may be all or a portion of the principal sum. Usually combined with accidental death insurance.

---

**dividend:** in life insurance, the annual refund of part of the premium paid on a participating policy after the company has set aside necessary reserves and made provision for claims and expenses. Also known as a policy dividend. Dividends are not guaranteed—so don't bet your life on them—but depend on the company's investment earnings, expenses, claims and other factors, and may be increased or decreased at the discretion of the company. *See also* **participating policy.**

---

**dividend options:** ways in which policy dividends can be paid. These include cash, a premium reduction, conversion into a paid-up addition to the sum insured or some other form of additional coverage. Or they can be left to accumulate in an interest-bearing cash deposit.

---

**double indemnity:** double your money, double their funds—a clause in life insurance providing the beneficiary with double the face value if the policyholder dies by accidental means. Made infamous

by Fred MacMurray and Barbara Stanwyck in the
movie of the same name. *See* **accidental death
benefit.**

---

**dread disease policy:** Tact is not one of their
strong suits. Health insurance that covers a maximum
of medical expenses arising from specified diseases,
such as cancer.

---

**earned premium:** the expired portion of a
premium. For example, if you pay for a policy for one
year in advance, then after three months that policy has a
three-month earned premium. The unearned premium is
the amount you have paid for coverage that has not yet
elapsed. You could call this "bought time."

---

**effective date:**   date when an insurance policy goes
into effect. Typically, a policy becomes effective when it
has been delivered to the applicant and the first
premium has been paid, assuming there has been no
change in the individual's insurability since the time of
application. Companies' practices vary significantly in this
area. Some policies are issued on a conditional-receipt
basis, and the applicant pays a premium with the application: if the insurance is assessed at standard rates,
the coverage will begin at the time set out in the receipt
rather than when the policy is delivered. Other companies provide unconditional temporary coverage until
the policy is approved for issue.

---

**elimination period:** the waiting period until
benefits start in a health and disability policy. Getting
better—or, alternatively, dying—eliminates you from
consideration.

---

**endorsement:** a provision changing the terms and conditions of an insurance contract; for example, to increase or reduce the stated coverage. *See also* **rider.**

---

**endowment insurance:** type of whole-life insurance that pays the face value to the beneficiary if the policyholder dies before the policy is fully paid for. If the policyholder is still living when the policy is paid up, he or she receives the full face value. And a round of applause.

---

**evidence of insurability:** information requested by an insurance company to determine the acceptability of an applicant for insurance. May include a medical examination.

---

**extended term insurance:** a form of term insurance available as a nonforfeiture option (*see* p. 69) to the owner of a cash-value life-insurance policy who discontinues premium payments. It continues the coverage for the face amount for a certain amount of time; how long depends on the cash value.

---

**face amount:** what you see is what you get. The amount stated on the face of the policy that will be paid on the death of the life insured or at the maturity of the policy. Also known as the "sum insured."

---

**federally registered company:** a life-insurance company registered with the Department of Insurance in Ottawa and subject to federal regulation. *Compare* **provincial life-insurance company.**

---

**grace period:** the period, usually thirty or thirty-one days from the due date of a premium, during which the overdue premium can be paid without penalty and the policy remains in effect. Wait too long and you take your life into your own hands.

**graduated life table:** table of mortality probabilities used by an actuary in calculating premiums. . . and grave expectations.

**group annuity:** pension plan providing annuities at retirement to a group of people under the same contract, usually issued to an employer for the benefit of employees.

**group life insurance:** life insurance issued to a group of people under the same contract, usually without medical examination. Such group buying may result in lower premiums. May be issued to an employer for the benefit of employees, or under the umbrella of another organization, such as a professional association. United they stand, united they fall.

**guaranteed insurability:** contract rider providing the right to purchase additional insurance at stated future dates without evidence of insurability.

**guaranteed renewable:** the right of the insured to continue the insurance for a substantial length of time by paying the premiums and making no changes in the policy, although the insurer might change the cost of the policy. Usually found in health insurance.

**incontestability:** once two years have elapsed from the date of a policy's issue, a life-insurance company cannot contest the payment of insurance monies, as it might if you died within that period and there was a suspicion of fraud or suicide or a lack of insurable interest. After two years, these are what are known as dead issues.

---

**individual life insurance:** life insurance issued to an individual. *Compare* **group life insurance.**

---

**installment refund annuity:** type of annuity guaranteeing an income for life. If the annuity holder dies before receiving the full amount of the premium paid in, payments will continue to the individual's beneficiary until the full amount of the premium is reached.

---

**insurability:** an individual's acceptability for insurance. The underwriters determine whether you have the write stuff.

---

**insurance:** the pooling of individual risks of losses, catastrophes, accidents and health problems into protection for you and profit for the insurance companies.

---

**insured:** the individual insured under a policy, usually but not always the policyholder. Insuring—then killing—someone is a classic plot of the thriller film. See *Double Indemnity*, the movie rather than the definition, for drama larger than life insurance.

---

**irrevocable beneficiary:** person named as beneficiary with the provision that he or she cannot afterward be changed by the insured without the beneficiary's written consent. That written consent is also necessary if the owner wishes to temporarily assign the policy to someone else (for example, a bank) as collateral for a debt, surrender it for its cash value, or take a policy loan. With beneficiaries like that, who needs enemies?

**joint and last survivor annuity:** type of annuity providing periodic payments as long as either one of two people continues to live. In some annuity contracts, payments continue at the same level when one of the annuitants dies; in others, the payments are reduced. Usually bought by a husband and wife.

**joint insurance:** life insurance written on two or more persons, usually with benefits payable at the first death. *See also* **crisscross insurance, partnership insurance.**

**key person insurance:** known in sexist quarters as "key *man* insurance." Life or disability insurance bought by a company to cover a person, such as a chief executive officer or senior manager, who contributes substantially to the success of the business. Heavily insured is the head that wears the crown.

**lapsed policy:** policy terminated through nonpayment of premiums. The term is usually used to refer to policies terminated before a cash or other nonforfeiture value has been built up.

**level premium insurance:** life insurance for which the premium remains the same throughout the contract. The premium exceeds the actual cost of protection during the earlier years and is less than the actual cost in later years. Investment of the excess premiums paid in earlier years builds up a reserve, which helps keep the premium down in later years, when the insured is older, wiser and a greater insurance risk.

**level term:** term policy with the same face value throughout the contract. *Compare* **decreasing term insurance.**

**life insurance:** form of risk sharing under which the individual insured (the life insured) pays contributions to the insurer, who then reinvests them. Ultimately the insurer makes payments, depending on the nature of the policy, either to the insured, on the maturity of the policy, or to a beneficiary when the insured dies. *See also* **endowment insurance, term insurance, whole-life insurance.** Remember, nothing in life is free.

**loan value:** the amount of money that may be borrowed against the cash value of an insurance policy, at a rate of interest often but not always stated in the policy. Policies written before the great inflation of the 1970s and early 1980s used to offer such loans at bargain rates. These days, interest rates tend to be more realistic.

**maturity:** when a life-insurance policy's face value becomes payable. Nice if you can grow old together.

**mortality rate:** insurance lingo for the relative number of deaths in a given group of people during a given period of time—used to estimate the probability of your decease during the period covered by your policy. The even more charmingly named morbidity rate is the relative incidence of sickness or accidents in a given group of people during a given period of time, used in calculating premiums for accident and sickness coverage. Killing you softly with their words....

---

**mortgage insurance:** form of decreasing term insurance, bought specifically to pay off the outstanding balance of a mortgage on the death of the life insured.

---

**mutual life-insurance company:** life-insurance company owned entirely by its participating policyholders rather than by shareholders. Management is directed by a board elected by the policyholders. *Compare* **stock life-insurance company.**

---

**new money plan:** new form of whole-life insurance launched in the 1970s using current interest rates in the premium calculation. Compared to traditional whole-life policies, whose premiums are based on conservative long-term assumptions about earnings on investments, new money plans provide less expensive coverage—particularly when current interest rates are high. However, the amount of insurance or cost of premiums may subsequently be adjusted, either upward or downward, to reflect changing interest rates.

---

**noncancelable:** a policy that is guaranteed renewable at the premium stated at the date of issue.

---

**nonforfeiture value:** the value of a life-insurance policy when the policyholder discontinues premium payments. The usual nonforfeiture options include taking the value in cash; applying it to purchase "reduced" paid-up insurance or extended term insurance; or using it as security for a loan against the policy to continue premium payments as an automatic-premium loan. There will now be a short test.

---

**nonparticipating policy:** policy whose owner does not share in any surplus earnings, or policy dividends, distributed by the company. Typically less expensive than a participating policy, since the premium is set as close as possible to the expected cost of insurance.

---

**nonsmoker plan:** less expensive form of life insurance for individuals who have not smoked cigarettes for at least one year. If you are buying term insurance, rates can be dramatically lower because the lower mortality rates for nonsmokers suggest they have a better chance of surviving the term period. The difference is less significant in whole-life insurance plans, since nonsmokers aren't immortal (though they do believe that God is on their side) and since premiums for whole-life policies are strongly affected by interest-rate assumptions as well as by mortality expectations.

---

**ordinary life insurance:** *see* **whole-life insurance.**

---

**owner:** the owner of an insurance policy. The owner has the right to receive any benefits under it, change the beneficiary or assign or transfer ownership. Usually, but not necessarily, the insured.

---

**paid-up insurance:** life insurance on which all the required premiums have been paid. Reduced paid-up insurance is insurance for a reduced amount, available as a nonforfeiture option (*see* p. 69) to the owner of a cash-value policy who discontinues premium payments.

---

**participating policy:** policy whose owner shares in the surplus earnings distributed by the company through policy dividends. These dividends give policyholders the opportunity to "participate" in the success of a company. However, the premiums are generally higher than on a nonparticipating policy, and dividends are not usually guaranteed, since there is always the risk of sharing in the company's failures.

---

**partnership insurance:** insurance program under which each partner in a business insures the other in separate policies or in a joint insurance policy. (*See* **crisscross insurance**.) If one partner dies, the other(s) can afford to buy out the deceased partner's interest in the business from the heirs. The show must go on.

---

**permanent disability:** inability of the insured to resume his or her regular occupation as a result of accident or illness.

---

**permanent life insurance:**   alternative term for cash-value life insurance. For example, whole-life insurance and endowment insurance are types of permanent or cash-value life insurance. *Compare* **term insurance,** which has no cash component and provides protection only for the term of the policy. Fierce ideological wars rage between the proponents of "perm" and "term," with the latter having the better of the battle in recent years, some say because of the lower immediate cost. A permanent insurance policy represents an investment as well as a source of protection, and should be compared carefully with term insurance, as well as with other investments.

---

**policy:**   document issued by the life-insurance company to the policyholder or owner that states the terms of the contract. This policy bears a policy date, used to measure policy years and anniversaries to calculate due dates for premiums and dividends, and used to determine the policy's cash value.

---

**policy loan:**   made by a life-insurance company to a policy owner on the security of the cash value of a policy.

---

**premium:**   regular payment or payments a policyholder must make to keep a policy in force.

---

**primary beneficiary:**   person first in line to collect the insurance money on the death of the insured individual. Should the primary beneficiary die before or at the same time as the insured (*see* **common disaster**), the proceeds will go to the contingent beneficiary.

---

**principal sum:** lump-sum payment of benefits; for example, an accidental death benefit.

---

**provincial life-insurance company:** a life-insurance company incorporated provincially and operating under provincial license only. *Compare* **federally registered company**.

---

**reinstatement:** option to reinstate a lapsed policy within two years of the date of that lapse, unless the policy has been surrendered for cash or unless a nonforfeiture option has been exercised. Requires payment of overdue premiums and new evidence of insurability, as well as payment of any outstanding policy loan.

---

**renewable term insurance:** form of term insurance with the option to renew the policy when it expires without providing new evidence of insurability. At each renewal date (typically either annually or every five years), the premiums increase. Usually a limit is placed on the number of renewals, or a limiting age is imposed. But *see also* **term to 100**.

---

**rescission right:** consumer-protection clause giving the right to cancel an insurance policy within a stated period after the policy has been delivered, with full refund of premium payments. The period is usually ten days, hence the expression "the ten-day free look." Well, maybe one thing in life is free.

---

**rider:** a waiver, endorsement, paragraph or clause attached to an insurance policy to expand or reduce the stated coverage.

---

**settlement options:** ways in which the policyholder or beneficiary can opt to have the policy benefits paid, other than as a lump-sum payment. Popular settlement options include various types of deposit accounts or annuities.

---

**shareholder insurance:** an insurance arrangement in which two or more of the shareholders in a privately held corporation hold policies on each others' lives, typically in conjunction with a buy-sell agreement (*see* p. 176).

---

**single-premium whole life:** policy in which the entire premium is paid in one sum at the beginning.

---

**standard risk:** a person entitled to insurance at the standard rate, without special restrictions. A substandard risk is a person whose insurance risk is greater than normal due to health or other problems, and who can be insured only at a higher-than-normal premium rate. Rates on lion tamers and Evel Knievel available on request.

---

**stock life-insurance company:** company with share capital and shareholders. The board of directors is elected partly by shareholders and partly by participating policyholders, if any. *Compare* **mutual life-insurance company.**

---

**straight life insurance:** alternate term for permanent life insurance or cash-value life insurance.

---

**suicide clause:** standard clause in life-insurance contracts stating that if the insured person commits suicide within two years of the issue of the policy, only a refund of premiums will be made. *See* **incontestability**.

---

**superintendent of insurance:** the head of the government body supervising the insurance industry within each jurisdiction. There are both federal and provincial superintendents.

---

**surrendered policy:** policy that has been canceled or given up in exchange for either its cash surrender value (*see* p. 59) or a nonforfeiture option (*see* p. 69).

---

**term insurance:** temporary life insurance, with no cash value, payable only on the death of the insured, if that death occurs within the period covered by the policy. You pays your money and you takes your chances. *Compare* **permanent life insurance**; *see also* **renewable term insurance**.

---

**term to 100:** actually a special form of whole-life insurance that generates no cash value until you reach age 100. Less expensive than most cash-value life insurance, because the policy has no cash surrender value, but usually an expensive proposition all the same, and lacking the flexibility of nonforfeiture options (*see* p. 69). May be useful in estate planning, for the benefit of your heirs. Certainly not much use till you're 100; then what use will you be?

---

**underwriter:** the insurance company or group that underwrites or insures a particular risk. The term may also be applied to the individual within the company who chooses which risks the company is prepared to insure.

---

**underwriting:**   process of classifying the insurance risk of the applicant, determining whether the application will be accepted and working out the appropriate premium level.

---

**waiver:**   the deliberate relinquishment of a right. Any waiver in an insurance policy must be clearly expressed in writing.

---

**waiver of premium:**   *see* **disability.**

---

**whole-life insurance:**   protection for the lifetime of the person insured, with a cash-value component and, in some cases, dividends. Also known as ordinary and straight life insurance. *See also* **permanent life insurance.**

# CHAPTER FIVE

# Property and Casualty Insurance

**act of God:**  an occurrence beyond the control of human beings, for example, a flood, hurricane, earthquake or tornado. Also, a convenient excuse— rather along the lines of "The devil made me do it."

---

**actual cash value:**  the current value of an insured article at the time of its loss. Rarely as high as you'd like it to be.

---

**actual damage:**  damage that has occurred, as distinct from potential damage. Often far worse than you'd like it to be.

---

**additional insured:**  person covered by a policy in addition to the policyholder. For example, an automobile policy insuring anyone driving a vehicle with the consent of the insured.

---

**adjuster:**  person who investigates an insurance claim. May be employed by the insurance company, or may be an independent adjuster retained by the company for a fee. It is also possible for insured individuals to retain a public adjuster to represent their interests in negotiations with the insurance company. (Adjusters for all, but not necessarily justice for all.)

---

**apportionment:**  division of a risk, or loss, between two or more parties. For example, a loss may be apportioned between two or more insurance companies insuring the same risk, or between the company and the policyholder, or between two or more parties on the basis of their contributory negligence.

---

**appraiser:** person with special skills and knowledge in determining the value of a specific type of property, such as real estate, jewelry, automobiles and so on. May be brought in by an insurance company in the event of a claim to appraise the damage or loss.

---

**assigned risk:** risk not acceptable to a single insurance company and therefore assigned to insurers in a pool, with each participating company accepting a share of the risk (and of the premium).

---

**attractive nuisance:** a hazardous condition on your property that may entice children to be injured. For example, if you put a parrot in a cage on your front lawn and a child puts a finger through the bars and gets bitten, you may be liable, even though the child is trespassing on your private property. Polly want a lawsuit?

---

**automobile insurance:** insurance against losses arising out of the ownership, use or maintenance of an automobile, including damage to the vehicle itself, medical and hospital care for the insured and passengers and legal liability for bodily injury. *See also* **collision insurance.**

---

**average risk:** risk assessed as qualifying for insurance at the standard rate for that category of property. In insurance-underwriting language, a "below-average risk" is a situation of greater hazard, while an "above-average risk" indicates conditions that are less hazardous.

---

**binder:** receipt given to the purchaser of a new policy that insures the policyholder until the actual policy is issued.

---

**blanket insurance:** what Linus would like. In fact, it's a single amount of insurance that covers several items (although this could include your favorite blanket). Such policies are usually subject to the fulfillment of certain requirements.

---

**broker:** independent businessperson who sells insurance policies, usually from a number of different companies, and is paid a commission by those companies for each policy sold.

---

**casualty insurance:** a curiously imprecise term with an elusive meaning. Loosely used to describe an area of insurance that's not particularly or directly concerned with life and health insurance or fire insurance. It is applicable particularly to personal-injury insurance, but generally it includes liability, crime, robbery, burglary, and, in many instances, the surety business under its umbrella. Automobile insurance also falls into this category but is usually referred to separately. When you hear the term "property and casualty insurance," property insurance refers to those policies that include fire coverage; casualty insurance usually includes the rest.

---

**catastrophe:** in insurance terms, Bad Day At Black Rock: large loss caused by some peril that exceeds expectations of loss from that peril. For example, the tornado that hit Barrie, Ontario, in 1985 qualified as a catastrophe. Insurance companies may buy catastrophe reinsurance, and thus share the risk of a particular type of catastrophe with other insurers.

---

**claim:** under an insurance contract, a request for reimbursement of a loss. Also used to refer to the amount claimed. The claimant is the individual making the claim, either the insured person or someone making a claim against the insured person.

---

**coinsurance:** arrangement to share a loss, between insurance companies or between the company and the insured. For example, a coinsurance clause in property insurance may require the property owner to buy coverage up to a certain percentage of the property's total value, ranging from 80% to 100%. If the insured fails to do this, he or she in effect agrees to self-insure a proportion of *all* losses—in a ratio determined by the amount by which the property is underinsured. That ratio is calculated as follows:

$$\frac{\text{Amount of insurance carried (Did)}}{\text{Amount required by clause (Should)}} \times \text{Amount of Loss} = \text{Claim paid}$$

For example, on a building valued at $200,000 with an 80% coinsurance clause, a property owner is required to insure for at least $160,000. If he or she insures for only $80,000, he or she is underinsured by 50%, and will therefore be liable for 50% of *all* losses, large or small. So if the loss is $50,000, the owner would collect only half the amount.

$$\frac{\$80,000}{\$160,000} \times \text{Loss of } \$50,000 = \$25,000$$

And you thought insurance was a dull business.

---

**collision insurance:** type of automobile insurance that pays for damage to a vehicle caused by a collision with another car or an object, whether or not the accident is the fault of the insured. Does not cover bodily injury or property damage caused by the collision (for which, *see* **automobile insurance**). Usually subject to a deductible clause.

---

**combination insurance:** insurance policy offering two or more forms of coverage, which were originally included in separate policies. For example, a homeowner's policy combines fire insurance and insurance against theft and other risks. Also called a package policy.

---

**conjugal rights:** legal euphemism for the rights that a husband and wife have to each other's society, including sexual intercourse. Loss of such rights because of injury to one partner—for example, an injury caused by an automobile accident—may be the basis of a claim for damages payable by the insured's insurance company. May also be the basis of some conjugal fights.

---

**contributory negligence:** where negligence on the part of two or more persons contributes to an accident, the degree of negligence for each is usually apportioned on a percentage basis.

---

**damages:** a sum of money claimed or awarded as compensation for loss or injury.

---

**deductible clause:** basic amount the insured must pay for a loss before a policy makes reimbursement. In some policies, this deductible "disappears" as the size of the loss increases. Not to be confused with retractable claws, though both can make you wince.

---

**endorsement:**  form used to make any change on an insurance policy, such as replacing an old car with a new one. Such changes require the consent of insurer and the insured.

---

**exclusion:**  something specifically not covered by a policy. For example, most policies specifically exclude losses due to radioactive fallout, as well as many other rarely encountered perils. Obviously they haven't had close encounters of the Chernobyl kind.

---

**facility plan:**  arrangement between insurance companies in a particular area to pool the risks associated with policies not usually acceptable to an individual company. Under the plan, the company writing the policy transfers the risks to a "facility" underwritten by all the insurance companies in the plan.

---

**fire insurance:**  policy covering damage caused by fire, lightning and certain types of explosion (but not the "Big Bang"). *See also* **friendly fire.**

---

**floater:**  policy covering movable property for loss or damages, as long as it remains within the territory specified, be it Canada, North America or the world. For example, fur floater, jewelry floater and so on.

---

**friendly fire:**  a fire in its proper place, such as a fireplace, barbecue or oven. Insurance covers only hostile (uncontrolled) fire; if you can't take *that* heat, get out of the kitchen.

---

**fur floater:**   *see* **floater.**

---

**hazard:**   anything that may increase the possibility of loss, harm or liability. Underwriters evaluate these hazards, then calculate the risks involved. Hazards may be physical—for example, the storage of inflammable materials in a building—or moral—for example, the mental attitude of the person insured. An individual with a criminal record for arson, for example, would represent a moral hazard; to insure such a candidate *would* be playing with fire.

---

**homeowner's policy:**   a combination policy providing protection against fire, theft, liability and other losses to which a homeowner is exposed.

---

**indemnify:**   to reimburse the insured for a financial loss. Most property and casualty policies are forms of indemnity insurance.

---

**inherent vice:**   the very nature of some goods (not to mention some people) that causes their deterioration, and therefore makes them uninsurable. For example, milk sours, metals rust. That's the way the cookie crumbles.

---

**insurable interest:**   a person must have sufficient interest in the item being insured to cause him or her a monetary loss should it be damaged or destroyed. An owner or a lessee would possess such an interest.

---

**insurable risk:**   risk an insurance company is prepared to insure against. You can be sure it's a calculated risk.

---

**jewelry floater:**   *see* **floater.**

---

**liability insurance:**   insurance against legal liability for injuries or damages to property of others. Just
as there are many reasons for being sued, so too are
there many forms of liability coverage, including
automobile liability, homeowner's personal liability,
manufacturers' product liability and contractual
liability. Suit yourself.

---

**liability limits:**   the maximum amount payable
by the insurance company under a liability policy. As
liability limits increase, so do premiums, but not
necessarily in proportion. Court awards for liability
in some cases exceed the amount stipulated in the
insurance policy concerned. Review your policy
periodically to make sure you can pull the coverage
over *your* head.

---

**libel insurance:**   insurance generally for the protection of persons working in the mass media against
court judgments arising from libel suits.

---

**Lloyd's:**   the mecca of the insurance world. A group
of individuals (*not* insurance companies) who form
syndicates to personally share liability for various insurance risks brought to them by Lloyd's brokers. Syndicates are represented by underwriters who do business at "the Room" in London, England. The corpora-

tion known as "Lloyd's of London" controls the membership, provides the facilities and serves the tea. One lump sum or two?

---

**loading:**  an amount added to the basic insurance rate, over and above that required for coverage of the actual risks insured, to cover the insurer's administrative costs. In some cases, refers to the amount added to the basic premium to cover an additional peril. Loaded down is how you will feel—loaded is how you'll want to get.

---

**loss:**  term used in insurance for all claims paid out, whether for an actual loss of property, for damage leading to a reduction in the value of property or for damages paid to a third party under a liability policy. (The insurer and the insured are the first and second parties.)

---

**merit rating:**  an individual's record, used for calculation of premiums, particularly in automobile insurance. If you mar it, no merit.

---

**Montreal Convention:**  international agreement setting out the limits of liability of airlines on international flights for baggage losses and payments for bodily injury or death. The convention increased the limits that prevailed under the previous Warsaw Convention. As you might have guessed, the sky's not the limit.

---

**named perils:**  not the perils of Pauline, though many of them might qualify. Specific perils against which a policy is issued. A named-perils policy protects *only* against the specified perils.

**non-owned automobile policy:** policy protecting an employer against claims arising from employees who use their own vehicles for company business.

**no-fault insurance:** type of automobile insurance that stipulates that, no matter whose fault an accident is, the victim collects damages and medical expenses from his or her own insurance company without an expensive process of claims adjustment and without lengthy litigation—the winner by no-fault. Already practiced in several Canadian provinces and in many jurisdictions in the United States. Fiercely resisted by insurers elsewhere, however, and also, of course, by lawyers.

**notice of loss:** requirement that policyholder sustaining a loss give immediate written notification to the insurer.

**overinsurance:** insurance in excess of the value of the item insured, whether through honest miscalculation or with the intent of defrauding the insurer. Many people have an excessive opinion of their worth.

**package policy:** *see* **combination insurance.**

**peril:** the cause of loss. For example, the fire, the explosion, the accident and so on.

**primary coverage:** where two or more policies cover the same item, the one that specifically covers the property that was lost or damaged is responsible for primary coverage and must first pay any loss. For example, a fur floater on a homeowner's policy is primary when the fur coat is stolen.

**proof of loss:** statement made under oath to the insurance company, setting out the insured's claim.

**rate:** cost of insurance per unit. (A unit can represent $100 of insurance or $1,000 of insurance.) The premium is the rate times the number of units of insurance purchased. For example, if a property costs $100,000, and the rate of insurance is $5 per $1,000, then the premium would be $5 times 100, or $500.

**rent insurance:** insurance for owners of rental property against loss of rental income under specified circumstances, such as fire.

**replacement value:** cost of replacing an article that has been lost or damaged beyond repair with one of the same kind and quality. Great way to update your stereo equipment—but don't take that as sound advice.

**risk:** the chance of loss. Sometimes refers to the subject of an insurance contract, as when talking of a "good risk" or a "poor risk." How you rank depends on how dangerously you like to live.

**schedule of insurance:**   list of items covered by a policy. For example, a list of cars insured under an automobile policy.

---

**settlement:**   claim payment made after the insurer and the insured have agreed, however reluctantly, on an amount.

---

**subrogation:**   right of the insurer (the first party) to pursue any course of action in the name of the insured (the second party) against a third party held to be liable for a claim paid by that company. For example, your insurance company may reimburse your claim for damage to your parked automobile, then attempt to recover the loss from the driver who caused the damage.

---

**third party:**   in insurance, the first party is the insurance company; the second party is the insured; and the third party is a person outside the policy who may be injured or whose property may be damaged. There can be many third parties in the same case. Third-party insurance protects against any loss any individual may suffer as a result of legal liability to others.

---

**tsunami damage:**   special insurance required by mortgage lenders for buildings in a tidal-wave zone. Not much call for it in Saskatchewan.

---

**underinsurance:**   insurance for less than the value of the property. Important where a coinsurance clause is involved.

---

**Underwriters' Laboratories:** an organization financed by insurance companies to promote fire prevention and safety by testing various manufactured items and approving those that meet their safety standards. An ounce of prevention is worth a pound of claim.

---

**uninsured-motorist coverage:** coverage providing damages for bodily injury or repairs to a vehicle resulting from an accident for which an uninsured third party is responsible. Included in most automobile policies.

---

**valuation:** appraisal of items to be insured, such as jewelry, furs and so on.

---

**war clause:** provision specifically excluding liability of the insurance company for losses caused by war, or by acts of hostility, even if war has not been declared. For example, the continuous bombings in Ireland, the undeclared war in Lebanon, Star Wars....

---

# CHAPTER SIX

# Investing in
# the Markets

**above par:** when a share is trading at a price greater than its par value, or the value assigned to it when it is issued by a company. Better on the market than the golf course.

---

**across the board:** widespread price movement, either upward or downward, in shares in companies in a particular industry, or in all sectors of the stock market.

---

**advances versus declines:** "advances" are the stocks that are trading higher than they were at the close of the previous trading day; "declines" are the ones that are trading lower.

---

**American Stock Exchange (AMEX):** second largest exchange in the United States, formerly the New York Curb Exchange. Less stringent in its listing requirements than the New York Stock Exchange.

---

**annual meeting:** yearly meeting at which stockholders elect the corporation's board of directors and vote on other matters, either in person or by proxy. Usually poorly attended, unless there's a good fight or an open bar.

---

**annual report:** yearly statement issued to shareholders and analysts to report year-end financial information, major developments since the last such statement and activities planned for the years ahead. Annual reports should be taken with several grains of salt (or several stiff drinks)—some are much better physically than fiscally.

---

**arbitrage:** the purchase of something in one market for simultaneous sale in another market, to take advantage of price differences (or "spreads") at the moment of purchase and sale. For example, if gold is selling for $340 an ounce in London and $341 an ounce in New York, the arbitrageur can buy in London to sell in New York and profit from the spread. May be applied to foreign exchange, foreign-exchange futures, securities, precious metals and a variety of other commodities. If this definition is all you know about arbitrage, keep it that way.

---

**arm's length transaction:** a transaction in which buyers and sellers are completely independent of each other. As opposed to a non-arm's length transaction, where buyers and sellers may be colluding to manipulate stock prices. A subject of intense interest to government regulators.

---

**authoritarian:** investment approach where you follow the advice of someone presumed to know better than you.

---

**average down:** to reduce the average cost of the shares you hold by buying more as the stock falls in price. For example, if you buy 200 shares at $15 and the price falls to $10, you can average down by buying 200 more, bringing your average price for the first 200 shares down to $12.50. If the price of the share moves up again, you will break even when it hits $12.50. If the share plunges further, you may have done a very silly thing.

---

**average up:** to average down in reverse gear.

---

**basis point:**  $\frac{1}{100}$ of 1%. Fifty basis points is $\frac{1}{2}$%. Even fractional differences are important in calculating bond yields. (For example, if one bond yields $10\frac{1}{4}$% and another $10\frac{1}{2}$%, the difference is 25 basis points). Also important in establishing the prime rate.

---

**bear:**  one who thinks the market will decline, and then bases investment decisions on that assumption; for example, short selling—selling securities or commodities one does not own in the expectation of a price decline. Possibly from the proverb about "selling the bearskin before catching the bear." The adjective bearish is applied to those inclined to think the market will decline. They almost always eat lunch alone.

---

**bear market:**  a market in which prices are generally declining. There is often disagreement among market watchers about how long and severe a decline must be to qualify as a true bear market.

---

**beta factor:**  a measure of the average percentage change in the price of a stock or group of stocks relative to that of a market index over the same period of time. Typically, the higher the beta, the more volatile the stock.

---

**bid/ask price:**  the bid price is what the buyer is willing to pay. If it is less than the seller's asking price, there is no deal.

---

**Big Board:**  the New York Stock Exchange.

---

**Black Tuesday:**  October 29, 1929, the day of the Wall Street collapse.

---

**block:**  a large amount of stock in round numbers, typically ten thousand or more.

---

**blue chip:**  a high-quality low-risk stock issued by a well-established company with a reputation for reliability, stability and the consistent payment of dividends. Favored by conservative investors, possibly including the apocryphal widows and orphans.

---

**board lot:**  the standard minimum lot traded on a stock exchange, usually set by the rules of that exchange.

---

**bond:**  an interest-bearing debt instrument, issued by a government or corporation that promises to pay the bondholder specific sums of interest at specified times, and to repay the face value on maturity. Bonds that are traded in the markets (as opposed to Canada Savings Bonds) fluctuate in value and may trade at a discount or premium to their face value, depending on the difference between the interest they pay and current interest rates. The amount by which the price paid for a bond is less than its face value is called the bond discount; the amount by which the price paid for a bond exceeds its face value is called the bond premium.

---

**bond rating:**  evaluation of the quality and riskiness of a bond. Put out by rating services such as Moody's Investors Services and Standard and Poor's. Makes provincial treasurers quake.

---

**book value:** the value of a company's assets as carried on its books. Most stocks trade above their book value.

---

**broker:** a registered agent who may buy and sell securities, commodities and other properties on behalf of clients for a commission. In hard times, they do a lot of telephoning.

---

**bull:** one who expects the market to advance forcefully. Bullish describes those who are optimistic about market prices. They never eat lunch alone.

---

**bull market:** a market in which the general price trend is upward over a long period of time. Bull markets, like time, heal most mistakes. And you can buy late and still make money.

---

**buy order:** instruction to your broker to buy a particular number of shares of a particular stock.

---

**call:** an option contract giving you the right to buy a fixed amount of a specified stock at a specified price within a given period of time. Those who purchase calls believe that the price of a stock will go up before the expiration of the option, allowing them to resell the contract at a profit. The reverse of a put.

---

**capital gain:** the amount by which the price you sell a security, commodity or other property exceeds the buying price. What you hope to make when you invest. The opposite of a capital loss.

---

**capital markets:** securities markets trading in stocks and bonds.

---

**Canadian Over-The-Counter Automated Trading System (COATS):** computerized system that lists quotes for Ontario stocks traded over the counter.

---

**commission:** the fee charged by brokers for buying and selling securities or commodities on the customer's behalf.

---

**common stock:** shares that represent an ownership interest in a company and that usually but not always convey voting rights. Common stockholders assume some risk, in the sense that the company must pay all other debts—including the dividends due to preferred shareholders—before declaring a dividend on common stock. But if the company does well, the common stockholder stands to gain more in terms of capital appreciation and dividends.

---

**convertible bond:** bond that the holder has the option of converting into other securities of the corporation, such as stocks, when such an exchange becomes advantageous.

---

**convertible preferred stock:** preferred shares that can be converted into common stock.

---

**coupon:** certificate attached to a bond that is clipped and presented for interest payment on the due date.

---

**cumulative preferred:** preferred stock in which dividends that are not paid in a particular year will be paid in subsequent years before any dividends are paid to common shareholders.

---

**day order:** an order to buy or sell a particular security, valid only for the day on which it is given.

---

**dealer:** one who buys for his or her own account and resells from that inventory, as opposed to a broker, who merely represents buyers and sellers. A brokerage firm may act as either broker or dealer, depending on the transaction. Most dealing is in over-the-counter securities not actively traded on a major stock exchange.

---

**debenture bond:** a corporate or government bond backed up by the credit standing of the issuer rather than secured by any specific collateral.

---

**depression:** period of economic decline, more severe and long-lasting than a recession. In a depression, there is very high unemployment; businesses fail, major economic institutions collapse, market prices decline and visits to the shrink increase. The last depression was in the 1930s, although 1981–1982 tested the definition of "recession" to the limit.

---

**discount brokerage:** service on which you pay a lower rate of commission on security transactions than you would through a full-service brokerage firm.

---

**discretionary account:** one in which an authorized broker may buy and sell securities on your behalf, within certain agreed limits, without consulting you.

---

**dividend:** payment per share held, determined by the corporation's board of directors.

---

**Dow Jones Averages:** indexes of the average share prices of major corporations trading on the New York Stock Exchange, grouped under industrials, transportation and utilities. The industrial index, based on just thirty corporations, is most widely followed as an indicator of the overall health of the market.

---

**earnings per share (EPS):** a company's net after-tax earnings, less preferred stock dividends, divided by the number of shares of outstanding common stock. Investors examine earnings per share in relation to previous years' earnings, stock price and other variables to identify undervalued stocks.

---

**equity:** shares of ownership in a corporation, either common or preferred stock.

---

**Eurobond:** a corporate bond issued through international financial markets, payable in the currency in which the bond is issued.

---

**Eurodollars:** U.S. dollars held on deposit in banks throughout the world and used for trade financing.

---

**exchange rate:** the rate at which one currency can be exchanged for another at any given time.

---

**ex-dividend:** without dividend. Cash dividends on stocks are typically paid quarterly. If you buy a stock before the ex-dividend date, you collect the dividend for that quarter, but if you buy it after it has "gone ex," you are buying it without the dividend. The share price may reflect the difference.

---

**face value:** the amount printed or stamped on an instrument of value, such as bonds, insurance policies, coins, bank notes and so on. The face value of bonds is also called the par value; it is the value on which interest is calculated and at which the bond is redeemed on maturity, if the issuer has not defaulted.

---

**fall out of bed:** what a market does when it plunges far below recent levels. Recession is when it stays on the bedroom floor. Depression is when it goes through it.

---

**Federal Reserve Board:** the board of governors administering the U.S. Federal Reserve System. Its duties include setting bank-reserve requirements, market-margin requirements and discount rates, and controlling overall money supply. Because of its tremendous influence over U.S. and world markets, its every move is closely watched. Known as "the Fed."

---

**fiscal year:** a corporation's accounting year, often different from the calendar year.

---

**floor:**   trading area of a stock exchange.

---

**floor trader:**   employee or member of a stock exchange who executes buy and sell orders on the floor for clients of his or her own firm, or for those of other brokers. Watch a group of them at work. The scene can resemble feeding time in the shark tank.

---

**formula investing:**   investment by a predetermined plan. One example is dollar-cost averaging, in which you buy, say, $1,000 worth of a particular security every quarter, no matter what its current price. The aim of such approaches is to simplify the investment process.

---

**front-end load:**   sales charge placed on a mutual fund at the start of the contract to purchase shares. (In a no-load fund the shares are sold without such markups.) The size of the front-end load can vary from fund to fund. If buying, you should ask a loaded question.

---

**fund:**   commonly refers to a mutual fund. Also: to supply capital or to make provision for the payment of debt.

---

**fundamental analysis:**   method of selecting stocks for purchase based on a broad spectrum of financial and economic data, including the value, quality and yield of a corporation's shares and the corporation's prospects for growth in the light of prevailing economic conditions. *Compare* **technical analysis.**

**futures:** a contract to buy or sell with delivery set at a specified future date. Futures may be purchased on stocks, commodities and foreign currencies. Changes in the market price between the contract date and the delivery date produce the trader's profit or loss. In some cases, futures are bought with the full intention of accepting delivery. For example, a corporation that will need to pay for an import shipment in U.S. dollars in three months locks in its costs in terms of the U.S. dollar by buying currency futures now. In other cases, the contract is bought for speculative purposes. For example, a trader buys futures in pork bellies in the belief that they will rise in price, resell at a profit and bring home the bacon.

---

**futures exchange:** an exchange for trading futures contracts.

---

**glamour stock:** stocks that have caught the public's eye, either through publicity or word of mouth, leading to heavy buying activity. When a company or industry becomes really glamorous, prices may rise to levels defying all logic. Today's glamour shares are often tomorrow's dogs, but big profits are to be made by those who get in and out before the crowds. Big losses are made by those who get in while the ins are getting out.

---

**gold certificate:** certificate issued by a financial institution that is convertible to gold bullion, the way real money used to be. A convenient way of holding gold, although scorned by true gold bugs, who'd rather bury the stuff in their back gardens.

---

**gold fix:** the setting of the price of gold by dealers, as in "the London gold fix."

---

**hedge:** to minimize your risks by making counterbalancing investments. For example, if you bought a stock at $100, you might simultaneously buy a put on that stock so you could sell it for $100 if the price should fall below $100 during the life of the option.

---

**holding company:** a company that owns the securities of another company or companies, usually with voting control.

---

**indicators:** economic measuring tools used to track how the economy is doing. They include leading indicators, which may offer a preview of the future; coincident indicators, which fluctuate simultaneously with economic activity; and lagging indicators, which confirm what has happened already. Investors pay most attention to the leading indicators, which include stock prices, corporate profits, new unemployment claims and consumer debt.

---

**insider:** an officer or director of a corporation. Because of insiders' access to inside information, their transactions in their own company's securities are closely regulated. Reports of such insider trading must be submitted each month to the provincial securities commission for inclusion in an insider report. Recommended reading if you're angling for the inside track. Or if you want to find out why your boss can afford a brand-new moss-green Mercedes.

---

**interest:** payment made to lenders for the use of their money.

---

**investor:** one who acquires securities or assets for the purpose of receiving income or eventual capital gain. As compared with a speculator, an investor is more concerned with safety of capital and minimization of risks than with maximization of potential profits.

---

**issue:** any of a company's securities. Also, the act of distributing new securities.

---

**junk bond:** a bond considered high risk because of its poor rating by the independent services, in some cases in default on interest payments. Can be more junk than bond.

---

**leverage:** the ability to make large profits with relatively small amounts of money. A conventional margin account for buying shares, for example, might allow you to control $1,000 worth of shares with a $500 payment. If the stock goes up, your potential profit is doubled. Of course, leverage is a two-edged sword, and if the stock goes down your losses are doubled, too. Investments in warrants, options and futures typically provide greater leverage than stocks and offer the potential for really big profits or losses.

---

**limited partnership:** arrangement in which investors in a business can enjoy certain tax advantages but are liable only to the extent of their investment. Limited partners do not participate in the management of the business.

---

**liquid assets:**   the assets of an individual or corporation that are in cash; items easily converted into cash.

---

**listing:**   stocks traded on major exchanges are listed securities, compared with unlisted or over-the-counter shares. To qualify for listing, a company must meet certain qualifications, more stringent for some stock exchanges than others.

---

**long-term investment:**   investment made with the hope of long-term growth in value or income rather than short-term profit.

---

**majority shareholder:**   a party owning sufficient shares in a company to have effective control. Once used only to describe those holding more than fifty percent of a corporation's stock, the term is now used more broadly to describe those who hold smaller percentages but still have effective control.

---

**manipulation:**   artificially creating trading activity in a stock to raise or lower its price, causing others to buy or sell. An illegal practice.

---

**margin account:**   account with a brokerage house allowing the investor to pay for a certain percentage of the market price of securities purchased, borrowing the rest from the broker and paying interest on the debit balance. The margin is the amount paid by the investor, with the broker holding acceptable securities as collateral for the balance of the purchase cost. Buying stocks in this way is known as buying on margin. Through leverage, buying on margin allows the investor to make a bigger profit if the price of the securities rises. However, should the price of the securities decline, the investor is liable to a margin call—a demand to put up additional cash or collateral to maintain the margin.

---

**market:** a place where buyers and sellers come together to trade, such as a stock exchange. Also, the supply and demand for a given security or commodity.

---

**market average:** the average price of a group of securities, used as a guide to the movement of the markets as a whole, for example, the Dow Jones Industrial Average, the TSE 300 Composite Index.

---

**market price:** the most recent price at which a security or commodity has been sold.

---

**market value:** the price at which an asset will sell in its market now. The market value of your securities, for instance, can be determined by multiplying the total number of shares you own by their current market price.

---

**maturity:** the date on which a financial obligation, such as a bond, becomes due for payment at face value.

---

**minority interest:** ownership in a corporation of insufficient shares to hold effective control. But you do get invited to the annual meeting. Lucky you.

---

**money market:** the financial market in which short-term financial obligations, or money-market instruments, are bought and sold. These instruments, typically with a maturity of less than one year, include Treasury bills; commercial paper, which are short-term certificates of indebtedness issued by corporations; bankers' acceptances, which are trade finance instruments guaranteed by a bank; and GICs (*see* p. 44).

**money supply:** the amount of a nation's currency in circulation and on deposit. There are various measures of money supply, all watched closely by sophisticated investors in the belief that money supply foretells economic trends, in particular a forthcoming increase or decrease in inflation.

**MSE:** The Montreal Stock Exchange.

**Moody's Investors Service:** an independent service, based in New York City, that publishes regular reports on stocks and bonds and is subscribed to by private investors as well as financial institutions. Bad reports can give rise to the Moody Blues.

**mutual fund:** a pool of investors' funds that is professionally managed and invested in stocks, bonds, options, commodities or money-market securities. The company that raises and manages this capital also goes by the name "mutual fund" (though it may, in fact, operate several funds) or by the term "open-ended investment company," because its capitalization is not fixed: additional shares are continually offered to meet public demand. Shares are not listed for trading on a stock exchange; they are sold, and bought back, by the fund itself. The twin benefits of diversification and sophisticated management are why more and more people want to join in the funds.

---

**NYSE:**   the New York Stock Exchange.

---

**nonvoting stock:**   typically, common stock with no or, in some cases, limited voting privileges. A number of Canadian companies issue two classes of common stock: those with full voting rights and those with none. Voting privileges allow a shareholder to participate in the election of directors, the appointment of auditors and the approval of major policy changes. However, most recent issues of nonvoting stock incorporate a takeover-protection provision that allows the nonvoting stock to convert into voting, in the event of a successful takeover bid for the company's existing voting stock.

---

**odd lot:**   stocks traded in less than an exchange's standard unit, which is normally a board lot of 100, and typically traded by small investors. The odd-lot theory suggests doing the opposite of what the odd-lotters are doing at any point in time, on the principle that the small investor is always wrong.

---

**officer:**   a member of corporate management able to act for the company within certain legal limits.

---

**open order:**   an order to buy or sell a security at a specified price, valid until filled or canceled. Also known as GTC—good till canceled. *Compare* **day order.**

**option:**   the right to buy (call) or sell (put) a fixed amount of a certain stock at a specified price within a specified time. Those who purchase options believe that the price of a stock will go up or down before the expiration of the option, allowing them to resell the option at a profit. If you call the price movement wrong, you are out of the money.

---

**over the counter** (OTC):   way of issuing and trading in securities for companies not able to meet the listing requirements of a major stock exchange. The over-the-counter market is made up of dealers who may or may not be members of a stock exchange, and is carried on primarily over the telephone. The unlisted shares that trade in this market will typically have less liquidity than those listed on the stock exchanges. Bond trading in Canada also takes place over the counter.

---

**par value:**   on common stock, the value assigned to it when it is issued. However, this figure has little or no relationship to market value, and "no-par-value" stock is now quite common. In the case of preferred stock, par value is more significant; it indicates the amount the investor would be entitled to if the company was wound up. Dividends on preferred stock are normally calculated as a percentage of par value. In the case of bonds, par value (equal to face value) represents their value when issued as well as when redeemed; also used in determining bond interest.

---

**penny stock:**   low-priced, speculative issues, trading over the counter or on a regional stock exchange with less stringent listing requirements than the TSE or the NYSE. The rule of thumb used to be that anything selling for less than a dollar was a penny stock, but inflation has pushed that figure up to three dollars. Betting on the pennies is like betting on the ponies— usually very risky, but with enough occasional winners to keep them coming back for more.

---

**portfolio:**  the total investments of an individual or institution. A portfolio can, and should, contain a variety of investment instruments.

---

**preferred stock:**  share in a company giving its owners certain preferences over common shareholders, such as a fixed-rate-of-return dividend and return of the stock's par value in a liquidation. Preferred shares are usually nonvoting, except when the dividend is suspended.

---

**premium:**  the amount by which a preferred stock or bond sells above its face, or par, value. In the case of a newly issued stock or bond, the amount by which the market price rises over the initial selling price.

---

**price/earnings ratio (P/E ratio):**  the ratio of the price at which a stock is trading to its earnings per share. A company earning two dollars a share and trading at sixteen dollars a share is trading at eight times earnings, with a P/E ratio of eight.

---

**prime rate:**  the interest rate charged by major banks to their most creditworthy corporate customers. Prime rate is used in setting other interest rates, and is viewed as a good indication of economic conditions.

---

**principal:**   the amount of money you've invested, on which interest or dividends may be paid.

---

**pro rata:**   in proportion to. A dividend is a pro-rata payment, because the amount a shareholder receives is in proportion to the number of shares owned.

---

**prospectus:**   a legal document describing securities being offered for sale to the public and prepared in accordance with the requirements of the provincial securities commission for full disclosure.

---

**proxy:**   written authorization given by the shareholder to someone else, who need not be a shareholder, to vote his or her shares at a shareholders' meeting. Usually shareholders delegate their votes to management of the company in this way. In a contest between factions of shareholders, a proxy fight may ensue.

---

**Prudent Man Rule:**   provincial law requiring that a person controlling investments for others, such as a trustee, use discretion and conservatism and avoid all forms of speculation, acting only as a prudent person would. In some provinces, trustees may invest only in a list of securities designated by the province.

---

**put:**   option contract giving you the right to sell a fixed amount of a certain stock at a specified price within a specified time. Those who purchase puts think the price of the stock will go down before the expiration of the option, allowing them to sell the option at a profit.

---

**quotation (quote):** the highest bid to buy and the lowest offer to sell a security at a given time.

---

**random walk theory:** the idea that, because stock prices are unpredictable, you can do as well buying stocks at random as on any more studied basis. The opposite of fundamental analysis and technical analysis.

---

**recession:** periodic low in the business cycle, accompanied by high unemployment, lower corporate profits and declining stock prices. A recession is said to exist when a country's gross national product (or gross domestic product, as Ottawa now terms its economic yardstick) declines for more than two quarters in succession.

---

**recovery:** period of advancing prices following a decline in the markets.

---

**registered representative:** a salesperson employed by a brokerage house and registered with the provincial securities commission.

---

**retractable bond:** a bond issued with a specific maturity date that allows the holder the right to redeem it at an earlier preset date.

---

**rule of 72:** a way to calculate the return on an investment. To determine how long it will take you to double your money at a fixed rate of interest, divide 72 by the interest rate. For example, at 12%, it will take approximately six years (72 ÷ 12).

---

**securities:**   generic term for pledges such as stocks (equity securities) and bonds (debt securities) issued by corporations to raise funds. Equity securities represent claims of owners and debt securities represent claims of creditors; neither is necessarily secure.

---

**Securities Act:**   provincial act, administered by the securities commission in each province, setting down the regulations under which securities may be sold to the public.

---

**seller's market:**   market in which demand is high, causing prices to rise.

---

**shareholder:**   individual or organization owning shares in the ownership of a corporation. Also called a "stockholder." The shareholder's equity in a company is the amount by which assets exceed liability.

---

**short:**   to go short is to sell shares you do not own in the expectation that the market will go down. The brokerage firm lends you the stock for delivery to the purchaser. Later, you hope to buy the stock at a lower price to cover your short position and pay the borrowed stock back to the broker, paying the interest and broker's commission out of your profits. Should the price of the stock rise instead of fall, you will find yourself in a short squeeze.

---

**small investor:**   the average individual investor, buying from a few to a few hundred shares per transaction. Although they are the largest group of investors, small investors as a group are small potatoes since they hold fewer shares than institutions, corporations and sophisticated investors.

---

**sophisticated investor:** the wealthy individual investor with knowledge, experience and the time to study market conditions. He or she often invests large sums of money and moves more rapidly than institutional investors when opportunity presents. What every small investor would like to be.

---

**speculation:** an investment strategy involving the assumption of a relatively high degree of risk in order to realize substantial profits through such techniques as margin buying, leverage and short selling. As compared with investors, speculators usually seek short-term capital gain rather than regular interest and security of capital.

---

**Standard and Poor's:** independent advisory and stock-and-bond-rating service based in New York City. Compiler of the S & P Stock Price Index, which is based on issues traded on the NYSE and provides a broader measure of market movements than the Dow Jones Industrials.

---

**stock:** term used to describe equity shares in a company, either common or preferred.

---

**stock exchange:** organized marketplace for buyers and sellers of securities. Trading is restricted to members of the exchange.

---

**stock market:**   popular term for stock exchange.

---

**stop-loss order:**   an order to your broker to sell a stock when its price reaches a specified level—either to protect a part of your profit or to limit a potential loss. There is no certainty, though, that the order will be executed at the price level you specify.

---

**stripped bond:** government or government-guaranteed bond from which coupons have been stripped, so that no interest is paid, sold at a steep discount from face value at maturity. Also called zero-coupon bond.

---

**syndicate:**   group of investment dealers sharing the risks in underwriting and distributing a new issue of securities or a large block of an outstanding issue.

---

**takeover:**   when one corporation acquires another, either in a friendly merger or by unwanted grab. Can make feeding time in the shark tank look like a picnic.

---

**technical analysis:**   method of assessing a stock or the market in general by examining past movements in stock prices, stock volumes and other market indicators, rather than by studying the underlying economic fundamentals (*see* **fundamental analysis**). A technical analyst is also sometimes known as a chartist because of his or her reliance on charts of price fluctuations.

---

**tender offer:** request by a corporation for shareholders to surrender their stocks within a certain time period, typically at a price higher than the current market price.

---

**ticker tape:**  a service offered by major exchanges that reports price and size of security transactions. These reports are no longer spewed out on ribbons of paper, but are carried on electronic terminals. Gone are the days of throwing ticker tapes out of windows— or of finding windows that still open.

---

**trader:**  one who buys and sells stocks for short-term profit.

---

**Treasury bill:**  short-term federal-government debt, usually issued in large denominations and sold mainly to large institutional investors, though the small investor is welcome to buy. Also known as T-bills. Treasury bills do not pay interest, but are sold at a discount and mature at face value.

---

**treasury stock:**  authorized but unissued shares in a corporation, or previously issued shares reacquired by the corporation. Such shares have no voting rights and neither pay nor accrue dividends.

---

**TSE:**  the Toronto Stock Exchange.

---

**TSE 300 Composite Index:**  market average of the three hundred most actively traded stocks listed on the TSE, made up of fourteen subindices (transportation, oil and gas and so on), each of which represents a different sector of the economy. The most broadly based, closely watched Canadian market average.

---

**underwriting:** in the securities industry, the purchase of a security issue by one or more investment dealers, or underwriters, for resale to the public.

---

**unlisted stock:** *see* **over the counter**.

---

**VSE:** the Vancouver Stock Exchange. Less stringent in its listing requirements—but more sexy for speculators—than the TSE.

---

**venture capital:** risk capital invested by a venture-capital company in a new, expanding or financially troubled organization, typically in exchange for a minority shareholding.

---

**Wall Street:** generic term for the New York City financial district in and around Wall Street in Manhattan. Also called "the Street."

---

**warrant:** certificate that gives the holder the right to purchase securities at a specified price, usually within a specified time limit. Warrants are usually issued along with a new issue as an added inducement to investors.

---

**xd:** symbol used in newspapers and reports to indicate that a stock is trading ex dividend. Sometimes spelled "x."

---

**yield:** the return on your investment. To figure a stock's yield, you take its annual dividend as a percentage of its current market price. In calculating a bond's

CHAPTER SEVEN

# Personal Taxation

**accrual:** the accumulation of amounts owed but not yet paid out. For example, a Canada Savings Bond (CSB) of the compound-interest variety will continue to accrue interest until it is cashed. However, under the accrual rules introduced by the federal government in 1982, taxpayers must declare as income amounts earned from CSBs, insurance policies and annuities at least every three years and pay any taxes owing on that income, whether or not the income has actually been received. It may be advantageous to declare accrued interest more frequently than every three years, to take full advantage of the $1,000 investment income deduction.

---

**alimony:** allowance made to a former spouse for his or her maintenance after a divorce. Regular payments made under a formal separation agreement are deductible. For the recipient, they are taxable income, but he or she will probably pay tax at a lower rate than the spouse making the payments. Alimony could therefore be described as a special form of income splitting.

---

**allowable business investment losses:** special provision in the Income Tax Act for taxpayers who invest in their own incorporated business and suffer losses. Taxpayers in this situation may deduct one-half of the business investment loss against income from all sources. To be allowable, you must have taken the loss through the arm's-length disposition of your shares in the Canadian-controlled private corporation, or in the form of a debt owed to you by that corporation.

---

**allowable capital losses:** if your capital losses exceed your capital gains, then half of this net capital loss is your allowable capital loss. Net capital losses in excess of the allowable amount can be carried forward indefinitely, or backward for up to three years.

---

**appeal:**  if you dispute your income-tax assessment, you have the right to file a notice of objection with Revenue Canada. If you fail to get satisfaction in this way, you may then make an appeal to the Tax Court of Canada (formerly the Tax Review Board) or to the Federal Court of Canada. Decisions of the tax court can be further appealed, all the way up to the Supreme Court of Canada. Of course, you may get there only to have your objection overruled.

---

**appreciation:**  an increase in the value of an asset. Depending on the nature of the asset, you may be liable to pay tax on your capital gain when you sell it.

---

**assessment:**  following the processing of your tax return, you will receive a notice of assessment, either agreeing or (more rarely) disagreeing with your calculation of taxes payable. But *see also* **reassessment**—the taxman sometimes rings twice.

---

**attribution rules:**  *see* **income attribution rules**.

---

**audit:**  examination of your records, at the discretion of Revenue Canada. An audit may be directed at all taxpayers falling within a certain occupational group, or with some other distinctive quality in common—for example, investment in the same tax shelter—or it may be specifically directed at you because of questions left unanswered by your tax return. Fear of audit ranks right up there with fear of flying. But in this case, you wonder whether your numbers are going to fly.

---

**averaging:**  provision to ultimately reduce or level the tax impact of a large increase in income in a particular year. The only form of averaging now permitted is forward averaging, which allows you to place a chunk of your current income in a notional account to be carried forward into future years. A lower tax rate will apply to your now-reduced current income, but you must still pay the highest applicable tax on the forward-averaged amount in that year as well. You can then elect to claim all or part of the amount carried forward as income in a year when you expect your earnings—and tax rate—to be lower. At that time, you can also claim a credit for the tax previously paid on the forward-averaged amount. The net result could be a refund in your low-income year. This is Revenue Canada's idea of a big break.

---

**balance due:**  the final verdict—unless you're getting a refund. Psychologically, the bottom line in your tax return (although "amount enclosed" and your signature and address come below it).

---

**barter:**  inefficient form of doing business, sometimes promoted as a way of avoiding tax. Actually, Revenue Canada regards barter transactions as fully taxable, except where they occur on an amateur basis. Suppose, for example, that you are an accountant and your next-door neighbor is a dentist. If you performed accounting services in exchange for dental services, you would be obliged to include the value of those dental services in your income. If, on the other hand, you swapped your home-grown apples for the dentist's pears, the transaction remains nontaxable, since neither of you is a professional gardener. By the same token, you could work on the dentist's teeth and he could complete your tax return. (He'd end up with filed incisors, you with an improved tax bite.)

---

**benefits:**   *see*   **employee benefits.**

---

**business losses:**   losses incurred by an unincorporated business are deductible for tax purposes against income from other sources, such as employment income, assuming that the business has a "reasonable expectation of profit." Many part-time businesses lose money, especially in the first few years, once all deductible business expenses are taken into account. Indeed, many individuals who fail to report income from a part-time business may in fact be failing to report a loss that would reduce their overall tax burden.

---

**Canada/Quebec Pension Plan** (CPP/QPP): CPP/QPP contributions are deductible from taxable income. Payments do not qualify for the pension income deduction.

---

**capital cost allowance** (CCA): a deduction against income to cover depreciation in the value of an asset that is used to earn income, such as an investment property. Based on the theory that assets, like beauty, lose value over time due to use, wear and tear and aging. The amount that may be deducted depends on the nature of the asset. The rate for most buildings, for example, is 2½% of the original cost of the asset in the first year, 5% of the remaining balance (which is known as the undepreciated capital cost) in the next, and so on. An automobile used for business purposes, however, depreciates at 30% per year, and some tax shelters have, in the past, offered write-offs as high as 100%. (*See* **motion picture tax shelter**.) Should the asset be sold for an amount in excess of its undepreciated capital cost, this excess amount must be included in the taxpayer's income as recaptured capital cost allowance (or recapture). Since the death of an individual can trigger a deemed disposition of his or her assets, and therefore a recapture of capital cost allowance, it's important to look carefully at this subject from an estate planning perspective. (*See* Chapter 9.)

**capital gain:**   the profit on the sale of an asset sold for more than its purchase price, taxable at one-half the normal tax rate. Some assets are exempt from tax on capital gains, such as a principal residence. At one time, if you sold Canadian shares and bonds, up to $1,000 of the taxable portion of the gain could qualify for shelter under the investment income deduction. This has been eliminated by the capital gains exemption. However, in 1987, the first $50,000 of taxable capital gains qualifies as tax-free under the capital gains exemption, provided the taxpayer has not used a portion of this exemption in an earlier year. The amount of this exemption will increase steadily to a lifetime maximum of $250,000 by 1990. Take advantage of it: nothing ventured, nothing gained. For details on the implications of capital gains tax for estate planning, *see* Chapter 9.

**capital loss:**   loss on the sale of an asset. One-half of capital losses realized in any year may be deducted from taxable capital gains realized in that year. Where there is a net capital loss after you perform this cal-

culation, the excess loss may be deducted against taxable capital gains in past and future years. *See* **allowable capital loss.**

---

**carrying charge:**   cost associated with the ownership, rather than the acquisition, of an asset. Usually
synonymous with the interest payments on the loan
used to purchase the asset. For example, in the purchase of stocks through a margin account (*see* pp. 108–
109), the carrying charges are the interest payments to
the broker. Carrying charges are deductible for tax
purposes in many cases.

---

**charitable donation:**   you can deduct up to 20%
of your net income for donations made to a registered
charity or Canadian amateur athletic association. Give
and ye shall receive tax breaks.

---

**child-care deduction:**   expenses for child care deductible from the employment income of a working
parent for tax purposes, to a current annual maximum of
$2,000 per child and an overall maximum of $8,000. Can
be claimed only for children younger than fourteen, or
children who are physically or mentally infirm. Claimed
by the working parent who has the lower income.

---

**child tax credit:**   credit claimed by the spouse entitled to receive family allowance payments for an
eligible child. Designed to assist lower- and moderate-
income families, and granted according to a formula
designed to eliminate everyone else.

---

**commission:**   fee paid to a salesperson, agent or
broker for making a sale or purchase on another per-

son's behalf. Unlike ordinary employees, salespeople paid by commission are entitled to deduct expenses incurred in earning that income up to the amount of commission income received. This applies, however, only if they pay their own expenses, work away from their employer's place of business, are paid in whole or part by commission and receive no traveling allowance.

---

**company car:**   once a valuable fringe benefit, now not much of a perk at all. When reporting income, an employee with the use of a company car must include as a taxable benefit a reasonable stand-by charge for the car—typically two percent per month of its capital cost, although this may be reduced if the employee can demonstrate that personal use of the car was less than 12,000 km a year. Going nowhere *can* get you ahead.

---

**death duties:**   *see* p. 180.

---

**deduction:**   Elementary, my dear Watson, in foiling Revenue Canada. Certain expenditures are deductible from your gross income in calculating net income for tax purposes: for example, child-care expenses, RRSP contributions and so on. There are also some deductions permitted from tax payable, such as the child tax credit. The greater your powers of deduction, the lesser your net income.

---

**deemed disposition:**   under certain circumstances, a property is deemed to have been disposed of under the Income Tax Act, even though the property has not in fact been sold. As a result, there is a deemed realization of capital gains or losses, and taxes may be payable. Circumstances leading to such a deemed disposition include death (*see* Chapter 9) and taking up residence in another country (*see* **departure tax**).

---

**deferred profit-sharing plan (DPSP):** a type of profit-sharing plan that an employer institutes for employees (*see also* **employee profit-sharing plan**) to allow deferral of taxes on the distribution of profits. Contributions made to the plan and allocated on your behalf are not taxable as part of your current income; those allocations when paid—ideally, when you retire and your income drops—are taxable. A form of forced saving, one of the few that doesn't hurt. Yet.

---

**dental expenses:** may be claimed as part of medical expenses.

---

**departure tax:** special rules applying to taxpayers who cease to be resident in Canada. Departure, much like death, triggers a deemed disposition of all assets that could give rise to a capital gain or loss, with the exception of "taxable Canadian property," and any taxable capital gains must be included in the individual's final tax return. However, the category of "taxable Canadian property" is a very broad one, so that departure tax applies only to a very limited range of assets. Odds are that you can go without going broke.

---

**dependent:** the Income Tax Act allows a personal exemption for support of a dependent whose net income is below a specified minimum level. The most common exemptions for dependents are the married exemption for those who support a spouse, the equiv-alent-to-married exemption and the dependent child exemption. However, personal exemption claims are also available for the support of a variety of other relatives, including parents, grandparents, brothers, sis-ters, aunts and uncles. (What are you? A bear for punishment?) Dependents who are not children must be resident in Canada to qualify as exemptions.

---

**dependent child exemption:** deduction per-mitted to taxpayers who support a child during the taxation year.

---

**depletion allowance:** in accounting ter-minology, depletion is a reduction in the quantity of natural resources as a result of extraction. (Revenue Canada, for example, extracts tax and depletes *your* resources.) A depletion allowance is an adjustment to the accounts to reflect the cost of the amount of the natural resource that was depleted. To encourage oil and gas exploration, the federal government at one time allowed an individual taxpayer to deduct deple-tion against his or her resource profits. However, this deduction ceased for individuals in 1980.

---

**depreciation:** *see* **capital cost allowance.**

---

**disability allowance:** a personal exemption available if you, your spouse or someone for whom you have claimed an equivalent-to-married or depen-dent child exemption was totally blind at any time during the year or was confined to a bed or wheelchair due to illness or injury for a twelve-month period. Subject to restriction based on income of dependent.

---

**disposition:**   any transfer of an asset, either an actual disposition via gift or sale, or any deemed disposition.

---

**dividend income deduction:**   *see* **investment income deduction.**

---

**dividend tax credit:**   in calculating taxation of dividend income, your actual dividend income is "grossed up" by 33⅓%. A tax credit of roughly 22⅔% of your actual dividend income (not the grossed-up amount) is then deducted from the federal tax payable. The gross-up recognizes and allows you to include the pretax income of the company that is not reflected in the dividends; the dividend tax credit recognizes and allows you to subtract the percentage of tax *already* paid by the company on its earnings.

---

**divorce:**   messy in its tax implications, as in other ways. For the tax status of maintenance payments, *see* **alimony**. Individuals involved in a divorce should also pay careful attention to potential tax liabilities involved when they transfer property. Property may be transferred either at its adjusted cost base—basically, the purchase price—or at its fair market value at the time of the transfer. If the property is transferred at its adjusted cost base, no capital gains or losses are realized. However, the spouse receiving the property may face a hefty tax bill on capital gains if he or she sells the property later. If the property is transferred at its fair market value, the spouse who is transferring it must pay tax on any capital gains realized. One more thing for the lawyers—and spouses—to argue about.

---

**dues:**   union and professional-association dues may be deducted against taxable income. Regrettably, no such deduction is allowed for membership dues in a club whose main purpose is to provide dining, sporting or recreational facilities to its members. For a good time, don't call Revenue Canada.

---

**education allowance:**   deduction available to a student attending a post-secondary institution full-time. If the student does not require all or part of this deduction to reduce his or her taxable income to zero, the remainder may be claimed by a parent who provides support for the student. Behind every perpetual student, there's a grateful parent.

---

**eligible:**   in tax terminology, qualifying for specified tax treatment. For example, an eligible child is one who qualifies for the child-care deduction.

---

**employee profit-sharing plan** (EPSP):   plan through which a percentage of a company's profit is divided among employees. Contributions made to the plan and allocated on your behalf are taxable as part of your current income. However, you will not be taxed when you receive payment of those allocations. *See* **deferred profit-sharing plan.**

---

**employee stock option benefit:**   many employees are offered as an incentive the option to buy a fixed amount of stock in their company, at a fixed price or with a no- or low-interest loan. Once that stock option is exercised, any benefits you receive are taxable. However, through one of Revenue Canada's rare saving graces, you are allowed to deduct half that benefit. For example: you have an option to buy 1,000 shares in your company at $10 each and the price rises to $20. You exercise your option and buy the shares for $10,000; they are worth $20,000. Your profit is $10,000, but you pay tax on only half this profit, that is, on $5,000. The exception to this rule is stock options in the shares of a Canadian-controlled private corporation: you are not required to include such benefits in employment income when you exercise the option. But you will pay tax on the capital gain when you ultimately dispose of the shares.

---

**employment commission:**   *see* **commission.**

---

**employment expense deduction:** standard deduction, equal to twenty percent of earnings from employment (except director's fees) to a maximum of $500. You're allowed this deduction whether or not you actually incurred any expenses in connection with your employment, unless you're a commissioned salesperson claiming expenses against your commission.

---

**employment income:** income from employment includes salary, wages, commissions, director's fees, bonuses, tips, gratuities and honoraria. In distinguishing between income from employment and income from self-employment, the main criteria is the amount of control your company or supplier exercises over your work. Things get a little fuzzy in the case of salespeople, who may be judged either independent contractors or employees on commission income.

---

**equivalent-to-married exemption:** provision of the Income Tax Act allowing a single parent to claim the same exemption for a child as could be claimed for a dependent spouse.

---

**exemptions:** *see* **personal exemptions.**

---

**expense:** in business, an expense is a cost incurred for the purpose of earning revenue for a current rather than future period. For individual taxpayers, some allowable expenses that may be deducted against income also fall into this category. (*See* **child-care deduction** and **moving expenses**.) However, the category also includes personal expenses, such as charitable donations and medical expenses.

---

**fair market price:** normally, the value determined in bargaining between a buyer and seller; rarely as fair as either would like. For tax purposes, however, it is sometimes necessary to assess the fair market price of assets that are not actually sold, as in the case of a deemed disposition.

---

**family allowance:** payment by the federal government to families with dependent children. The family allowance must be included in the taxable income of the person who is claiming a child as a dependent. If the family-allowance checks are deposited in a separate account held in trust for the child, the interest earned by the account will be included in the child's income, but will typically not be large enough to create a tax liability.

---

**farm deduction:**  a farm can serve as a tax shelter because of the deductibility of losses from a farming business against other income for tax purposes. These losses may include capital cost allowance for the depreciation of buildings and equipment. However, where an individual's chief source of income is not farming, the losses that can be deducted are restricted to $2,500 plus one-half of any losses in excess of $2,500, to a maximum of $5,000. Moreover, to qualify for this deduction (a hobby farm, for example, does not), there must be a reasonable expectation of profit from the farming business in the future. In other words, will you make hay when the sun shines?

---

**federal dividend tax credit:**  *see* **dividend tax credit.**

---

**federal foreign tax credit:**  you may claim a deduction against federal tax payable for taxes paid on income or profits in other countries. A separate foreign tax credit calculation must be made for each country in which you are claiming the credit. The credit cannot exceed the amount of Canadian federal tax payable on the foreign income. (If you're in for the pound, they're in for the penny.)

---

**federal surtax:**  the taxpayer's nightmare—a tax on tax. Currently, it is three percent on your federal tax.

---

**federal tax:**  term applied to income taxes paid to the federal government. *Compare* **provincial tax.**

---

**flow-through shares:**   *see* **tax shelter.**

---

**forward averaging:**   *see* **averaging.**

---

**fringe benefits:**   the Income Tax Act once allowed companies to hand out to their employees a variety of nontaxable "perks" in lieu of additional taxable income. The golden days of perks are now over and, as a general rule, employees must now pay tax on most benefits from employment. A few fringe benefits, however, do remain tax-free, including up to $25,000 in group term life insurance; contributions on behalf of employees to group sickness or accident insurance plans; and extended medical and dental plans. Other benefits are beyond the fringe, though some may still be advantageous, such as company cars, employee stock option benefits and low-interest loans.

---

**gift tax:**   *see* p. 183.

---

**gross income:**   all income for a specified period, prior to deduction of expenses and other allowable deductions. *Compare* **net income.**

---

**income attribution rules:**   tax rules limiting the ability of a high-income earner to shift income to a spouse or child who has a lower tax rate. That'll teach you to pass the buck.

---

**income splitting:** spreading income among family members to reduce the impact of taxation (*see also* p. 184). A good way to keep it all in the family.

---

**income tax:**   tax levied on income.

---

**Income Tax Act:**   the legislation governing the administration of federal income tax.

---

**incorporation:**   the legal process of creating a corporation through which an individual or group of individuals form a legal entity with limited liability (*see* **limited partnership**). May be advantageous in some cases for self-employed taxpayers beyond a certain income level, since corporate income, particularly for small businesses, is typically taxed at a lower rate than personal income.

---

**indirect tax:**   tax on expenditures rather than on income. For example, sales tax.

---

**Indexed Security Investment Plan (ISIP):**   a registered investment plan that indexed the inflationary portion of capital gains on qualifying securities and exempted that portion from tax. Repealed in 1986.

---

**interest income deduction:**   *see* **investment income deduction.**

---

**investment income deduction:**   taxpayers are permitted to receive up to $1,000 in investment income tax-free each year. Qualifying investment income includes interest (*see* p. 107) from Canadian sources and dividends (*see* p. 102) paid by Canadian corporations.

---

**investment tax credit:**   credit allowing you to deduct a percentage of the cost of acquiring certain "qualified property," such as property used in mining or oil and gas exploration.

---

**limited partnership:** arrangement in which investors in a business have limited liability (meaning they are liable only to the extent of their investment) but can enjoy certain tax advantages. Limited partners do not participate in the management of the business. Limited partnerships are frequently employed in tax-shelter arrangements, such as nursing homes, hotels and leasing businesses, in which full capital cost allowance may be claimed, usually resulting in a loss for income-tax purposes in the early years of the investment. However, Revenue Canada has taken the position that a limited partner may not deduct a share of the venture's losses in excess of his or her liability to fund such losses.

---

**listed personal property:** most applicable to estate planning. *See* p. 186.

---

**lotteries:** lottery winnings, along with other gains resulting from gambling where chance is the determining factor and the odds of losing are high, are a form of nontaxable income. The government can afford to be generous because 999,999 times out of 1,000,000, your loss is its gain.

---

**maintenance:** *see* **alimony.**

---

**marginal rate:** *see* **rate of tax.**

---

**married exemption:** deduction available to a taxpayer who supports a spouse during the taxation year. The amount of the exemption is reduced by the net income of the dependent spouse above a certain level.

---

**maximum allowable deduction:** the upper limit on the amount you may claim under a particular deduction.

---

**medical expenses deduction:** where medical expenses exceed three percent of a taxpayer's net income, the excess may be deducted from income. To qualify, payments for medical expenses must be made to a medical practitioner, dentist or registered nurse. However, "medical" in this context covers a fairly broad range, including chiropractics, psychoanalysis, speech therapy and even Christian Science. And you thought politics made strange bedfellows.

---

**motion picture tax shelter:** tax break for investing in a certified Canadian feature film, once the most notorious of all tax shelters, now a shadow of its former self. An investor is now entitled to deduct only 50% of the cost of acquisition of an interest in a film in the year of acquisition (as compared with 100% prior to 1983) and must wait until the following year to write off the remaining 50%. Since an interest in a film can be acquired with an initial down payment of just 20% of your investment, with the remainder in the form of a promissory note, this shelter can still produce a significant tax saving in the short run. In the long run, however, you must pay tax on any revenue deriving from ownership in the film—if such revenue should ever materialize. Given the track record of Canadian movies, it is more likely that the film will fail to recover its costs. The investor, however, must still pay the amount owing on the promissory note. The tax savings achieved may then look rather less attractive. Are you sure you oughta be in pictures?

---

**moving expenses:**  deductible where a taxpayer is moving to a new location in Canada to take up employment or carry on business there.

---

**MURB:**  once-popular tax shelter involving Multiple Unit Residential Buildings that used the capital cost allowance to create a rental loss, which could be deducted against other income. (On rental buildings other than MURBs, capital cost allowance cannot be used to create a rental loss.) No new MURBs have been permitted since the end of 1981, although it is still possible to purchase an interest in an existing MURB.

---

**net income:**  your gross income, less expenses incurred to earn income, but before taxes are subtracted. On a personal tax return, net income assumes deductions for CPP/QPP, UIC and RRSP contributions.

---

**non-capital loss:**  loss from employment, property or business that may be deducted directly from taxable income, rather than being treated as a capital loss. For example, the loss on a rental property.

---

**nontaxable income:**  income not subject to tax. This includes gifts and inheritances; certain employee perks (*see* **fringe benefits**); proceeds from accident, disability or income-maintenance insurance policies, unless your employer has contributed premiums on your behalf; winnings from gambling (*see* **lotteries**); and various military-service pensions. In addition, certain forms of income paid in the form of an expense allowance are not taxable. They include traveling-expense allowances for salespeople and expense allowances for volunteer firefighters, elected politicians and clergy. In effect, pennies from heaven.

**objection:** *see* **appeal.**

**payroll deduction:** payment toward income tax, UIC, CPP/QPP and so on automatically deducted from your salary by your employer and forwarded to the relevant authorities. Form of withholding taxes.

**pension income:** income from any kind of a pension. Except for the Guaranteed Income Supplement (*see* p. 162), all pension income is taxable. *See also* Chapter Eight.

**pension income deduction:** the first $1,000 of pension income is deductible for tax purposes. This provision applies for taxpayers sixty and older to income from a pension fund (unless it is from a survivor or disability pension, eligible at any age), and from age sixty-five onwards to income from private sources, such as an individually purchased annuity (*see* p. 157) or RRSP (*see* p. 167). It does not apply to income from government plans, such as CPP/QPP and OAS (*see* p. 163).

**personal exemption:** deductions against taxable income allowed to individual taxpayers, such as the dependent child exemption and the married exemption.

**personal-use property:** most applicable to estate planning (*see* p. 186).

---

**political contribution tax credit:** the federal government and a number of the provinces allow a credit against taxes or a deduction from taxable income of a portion of contributions made to a registered political party. The maximum credit is currently $500. You'll have to decide whether you'll spend Liberally or be Conservative in your donation.

---

**principal residence:** a housing unit owned by a taxpayer, or jointly by a taxpayer with another person, in which the owner actually resides. May be a house, condominium, mobile home or even a houseboat. Ownership of a principal residence is perhaps the best tax break of all for ordinary Canadians, since capital gains realized on the sale of that residence are not taxable. If the owner moves out and rents the unit, it ceases to be a principal residence; however, tax is payable only on a portion of the capital gain when the unit is sold. That portion is equal to one plus the number of years during which the unit was used as a principal residence, divided by the number of years the taxpayer owned the unit. Since the notorious MacEachen budget of 1981, it is no longer possible for each spouse in a marriage to own a principal residence.

---

**profit-sharing plan:** payments made on your behalf into an employees' profit-sharing plan must be included in income; you must also include any income or capital gains they may earn within the plan. Payments from the plan, however, are not taxable. Different from a deferred profit-sharing plan, where con-

tributions into the plan are not taxable, but payments
from it are taxable.

---

**promissory note:**  common device in many tax
shelters to allow maximum leverage for investors. By
putting up twenty percent of an investment and signing a promise to pay the rest, the investor can immediately write off expenses associated with the full
amount of the investment. (*See, for example,* **motion
picture tax shelter**.) Good fun until the note comes
due—promissories aren't made to be broken.

---

**provincial tax:**  all provinces, along with the
Northwest Territories and the Yukon, levy their own
income tax. Except for Quebec, all provinces collect
the tax through the federal tax return, as a percentage
of the basic federal tax payable less certain allowable
provincial credits. Quebec requires its residents to file
a separate tax return. (That's separate, not séparatiste.)

---

**rate of tax:**  the more you make, the more they
take. Under a progressive income-tax system like ours,
the amount of income tax payable increases with the
amount of taxable income. To facilitate taxation,
Revenue Canada has grouped spreads of taxable income (say, from $18,240 to $18,250) into "tax brackets." Your marginal rate is the amount of tax levied on
your last dollar earned; it rises when your next dollar
earned pushes your income into a higher tax bracket.
If you're paying the top marginal rate, a marginal living
is what you'll be left with.

---

**reassessment:**  just when you thought it was safe
to go back in the water.... On processing a tax return,

Revenue Canada issues a notice of assessment indicating how much tax is owing or how much money is being refunded. However, it is still possible for the tax authority to change its mind, based on a closer examination of the records or new information, and reassess the tax owing. Normally, Revenue Canada has up to three years in which to reassess. However, there is no time limit on reassessment if the taxpayer has made any misrepresentation due to neglect, carelessness or willful default, or has committed fraud in filing the return.

**recaptured depreciation:** *see* **capital cost allowance.**

**refund:** what Revenue Canada hands back when you have overpaid tax, CPP/QPP or UIC contributions. What you always hope to get. Hope springs eternal....

**Registered Educational Savings Plan (RESP):** *see* p. 187.

**Registered Home Ownership Savings Plan (RHOSP):** until 1981, a tax break that allowed individuals who had never owned a home to deduct from their taxable income up to $1,000 a year for contributions to a registered savings plan. Sadly defunct.

**Registered Pension Plan deduction:** contributions to a registered company pension plan are deductible in determining taxable income. Substantial and significant changes to the rules have recently been announced. (*See also* Chapter Eight.)

**rental income:**  rents collected, less expenses, on an investment property. Where expenses other than depreciation exceed rents, the loss may be deducted from other income. Where rents exceed expenses, depreciation can be used to reduce the income to zero, although this depreciation will be recaptured when the building is sold. (*See* **capital cost allowance**.)

---

**reserve:**  a vehicle for paying tax on a cash-receipt basis. When selling an asset, you may structure the deal so that part of the purchase price is paid to you now and part in a subsequent year. In calculating the capital gain on the sale of that asset, you will usually be allowed to deduct a percentage of the gain as a "reserve," based on the actual amount still owing to you. Any reserve deducted in this manner in one year must be included when computing income the following year. A new reserve may be available based on the balance of the money still to be paid. Reserves are also allowed for other purposes, including allowing for the possibility of bad debts in reporting receivables (amounts owed to you) as business income. The idea is to spread out the tax bite.

---

**Revenue Canada:**  what the folks at the Department of National Revenue prefer to call themselves. We can't print what you'd prefer to call them.

---

**rollover:**  the transfer of property from one form of investment to another without triggering tax at the time of transfer.

**RRSP:**   Registered Retirement Savings Plan. Last of the red-hot shelters. A savings plan for retirement approved under the Income Tax Act, under which taxes are deferred on both the contributions and the income they earn until funds are withdrawn. For a rundown on the various types of RRSPs, *see* p. 167–168.

**scientific research tax credit:**   tax shelter that allowed corporations to sell to investors the investment tax credits the corporation would earn by carrying out scientific research. Mercilessly manipulated by a variety of slick operators, outright con artists and glorious eccentrics. Rapidly killed by Ottawa, but not before it had leaked millions of dollars in great exploitations.

**self-employed income:**   income from work over which you exert primary control. *Compare* **employment income.**

**share purchase tax credit:**   a tax break that allowed corporations to flow through their investment-tax credit to purchasers of qualifying new equity shares issued from June 30, 1983 to the end of 1986. Investors could then deduct their credit against federal tax in the year of purchase, or carry it back a year. Any unused credit could be deducted as a capital loss in a subsequent year.

**spousal tax credit:**   *see* **married exemption.**

**spousal transfers:**   does not mean that you can trade in your spouse for a newer model. It does mean, in computing taxable income, that you may transfer to your own tax return certain deductions your spouse has available but does not need to reduce his or her own taxable income to zero. These include the spouse's personal exemption for age, education, pension income, investment income and disability.

---

**stand-by charge:** in calculating the taxable benefit involved in use of a company car, the stand-by charge is applicable to those days in the year during which the automobile was available for the employee's personal use.

---

**stock options deduction:**  *see* **employee stock option benefits.**

---

**taxable allowance:** allowance paid by an employer that must be included in taxable income. Most personal and living allowances are taxable, although the Income Tax Act makes provision for certain forms of nontaxable income.

---

**taxable benefit:**  *see* **fringe benefit.**

---

**taxable income:** income from employment, from the conduct of a business or from investments. *Compare* **nontaxable income.** Now which would you rather have?

---

**taxation:** the imposition of a levy by government on individuals or companies, used to pay for public expenditures.

---

**taxation year:** individuals are taxed on a calendar-year basis. However, an individual carrying on an unincorporated business may choose a different fiscal period and thus a different year-end for that business. The taxpayer is then taxed each year on the income for the fiscal period of the business ending in that calendar year. (A fiscal period with a different year-end can be used to defer tax in the first year of operating a business.)

---

**tax avoidance:** in general terms, the avoidance of tax through legal as opposed to illegal means (*see* **tax evasion**). Revenue Canada, however, has its own definition. The department will accept what it regards as legitimate tax planning—that is, arranging one's affairs openly and within the framework of the law so as to defer, reduce or even completely avoid the payment of tax. However, it maintains a special Tax Avoidance Division (read "hit men") to scrutinize cases in which "the taxpayer has apparently circumvented the law, without giving rise to a criminal offence, by the use of scheme, arrangement or device, often of a complex nature, whose main or sole purpose is to defer, reduce or completely avoid the tax payable under the law." In other words, the department will look closely at transactions it disapproves of, to determine whether they successfully circumvent the law.

---

**tax credit:** a deduction from tax payable—for example, the dividend tax credit—as opposed to a deduction from taxable income—for example, charitable donation.

---

**tax deductible:** used to describe an item that may be deducted, as an expense, from taxable income.

---

**tax deferral:** many tax breaks (*see* **RRSP** and **motion picture tax shelter**) do not so much avoid tax on current income as postpone it. By deferring the payment of tax, however, the taxpayer hopes to be able to pay it, in the end, at a lower rate of tax. When a tax-deferral device expires, the taxpayer may defer payment further by a rollover into another tax-deferral instrument. Why pay today when you can put off till tomorrow?

---

**tax evasion:** acting with deliberate intent to deceive in reporting the amount of tax payable. Forms of tax evasion include concealment of income, fraudulent claiming of expenses or allowances and deliberate misrepresentation or withholding of relevant information. Tax evasion is, of course, illegal, and carries a fine of not less than twenty-five percent and not more than double the amount of the tax evaded, as well as the possibility of up to two years in jail. Penalties may be even heavier if the Department of Justice rather than Revenue Canada decides to get on your case.

---

**tax haven:** a foreign country in which little or no income tax is levied, such as Bermuda, the Bahamas, Grand Cayman and the Channel Islands. Paradise found.

---

**tax lien:** an encumbrance placed upon a taxpayer's property as security for unpaid taxes. (*See also* **lien**, p. 23.)

---

**tax planning:** arranging one's affairs so as to legally minimize or avoid the payment of tax. But *see also* **tax avoidance.**

---

**tax shelter:** an investment vehicle designed to achieve tax avoidance for the investor. Although income within the shelter is not taxable now, it may become taxable in the future. For example, flow-through shares are a popular, if somewhat risky, tax shelter, which "flow through" the exploration costs, and therefore the tax deductions, of a resource company to its investors. The tax cost of the shares is nil for now; when sold, any capital gain is taxable but could be further sheltered by the capital gains exemption. *See also* **tax deferral.**

---

**tax shield:** situation in which income that would otherwise be taxable is offset by allowable expenses.

---

**T1 General:** the standard individual income tax return.

---

**T1 Special:** simplified and shortened version of the T1 General tax return sent out by Revenue Canada to selected individuals, such as pensioners, whose reports are relatively simple.

---

**T4 slip:** statement of employment income provided by an employer.

---

**T5 slip:** statement of investment income.

---

**TFA1 slip:** statement of family allowance information.

---

**tuition fees:** fees for enrollment at a qualified educational institution, whether full-time or part-time, may be deducted against income.

---

**UIC:** Unemployment Insurance Commission.

---

**UIC benefits repayment:** required where you have received UIC benefits, and where net income for the year exceeds 150% of the maximum insurable earnings for the year.

---

**UIC benefits taxable:** all UIC benefits received must be included in taxable income.

---

**underground economy:** that part of a nation's economic activity that is neither recorded nor taxed. Includes barter as well as more subterranean pursuits. Drives Revenue Canada crazy.

---

**V-day:** Valuation day. The dates specified in federal income-tax legislation at which values for securities (December 22, 1971) and other assets (December 31, 1971) were determined on the introduction of tax on capital gains. Important only in the sale of an asset acquired prior to 1972.

---

**withholding taxes:** a tax deducted at source and remitted by the payor to the tax authorities on behalf of the payee.

---

**year-end:** *see* **taxation year.**

---

CHAPTER EIGHT

# *Retirement*

**actuarial assumptions:** used by actuaries in calculating the contributions required by a pension fund to meet its future obligations. These include assumptions about earnings from investments, salary levels, employee turnover and mortality rates. The good, the bad and the ugly.

---

**actuary:** specialist trained in probabilities and statistics who assesses the ability of a pension fund to meet its obligations. *See also* p. 57.

---

**ad hoc adjustment:** voluntary increase in the amount paid by a private pension plan to pensioners to compensate for declining purchasing power due to inflation. Made irregularly, and usually for considerably less than the full amount of inflation. In other words, if you're in hock, ad hoc won't help much. *Compare* **indexed pension.**

---

**annuity:** contract providing income payments at regular (usually monthly) intervals for a specified period. Some company pension plans of the money purchase type are geared toward the purchase of annuities. (*See* **defined contribution plan**.) They are also frequently bought from the proceeds of RRSPs (*see* p. 167), since the funds then become taxable only as payments are received. *See also* **annuity**, p. 58.

---

**benefit:** term applied to payments made under a pension plan.

---

**benefit formula:** the method by which an employee's pension is calculated under a pension plan, usually by multiplying some portion of the individual's earnings, or a fixed dollar amount, by his or her years of service. There are various benefit formulas, some more generous than others. In a best-average benefit formula, the final pension is a proportion of the individual's average earnings during a certain number of the highest paid years. A final-average benefit formula is based on the individual's last and typically best-paying years prior to retirement (anywhere from the last three to the last ten). A final-earnings benefit formula is based on the pay period (typically a year) immediately prior to retirement. In the less bountiful career-average benefit formula, the pension is based on the individual's average (as opposed to best) earnings over the entire period of employment. In a flat benefit formula, a fixed amount of pension is paid for each year of service, regardless of earnings. Ready to retire now?

---

**CPP/QPP:** The Canada Pension Plan (CPP) is a public contributory pension plan introduced in 1966; the Quebec Pension Plan (QPP) is parallel but independently administered. For the most part, the plans pay identical benefits, including death and disability benefits as well as a pension at age sixty-five. Both also permit payment of a reduced pension from age sixty onward. They are pay-as-you-go plans in which current payments are made out of current revenues, with no assets set aside to meet or fund future liabilities. (*See* **funding**.) Employers and employees each contribute to the plans. *See also* **integration with CPP/QPP.**

---

**cash withdrawal:**   *see* **return of contributions.**

---

**contribution limits:**   restrictions on the amount an individual may contribute annually to a Registered

Retirement Savings Plan. We would tell you what they are, but the federal government keeps changing its mind on us.

---

**contributory pension plan:** any pension plan to which both employees and employer contribute. Contributions are usually tied to earnings. *Compare* **noncontributory pension plan.**

---

**current service:** employee's length of employment while a member of a company's pension plan, used in the benefit formula to calculate the pension due.

---

**death benefit:** in a pension plan, the amount paid to survivors in the event that a pension-plan member dies before the pension commences.

---

**deferred pension:** a life annuity payable at some future date to an employee whose membership in a pension plan has been terminated before the normal pensionable age but too late to request a return of contributions. Payments usually commence when the employee reaches pensionable age. Also called a deferred annuity. *See also* **locking in, vesting.**

---

**defined benefit formula:** any benefit formula specifying, for a given level of income and period of service, the amount of pension payable. (*See* **benefit formula**.) A defined benefit plan is a pension plan providing a pension whose amount is determined by a defined benefit formula. Now you, too, can be a pension consultant.

---

**defined contribution plan:** a pension plan in which employee and employer contributions are fixed, for example, five percent of salary. The pension is based directly on the amount of contributions plus pension-fund earnings. Also known as a money purchase plan, since contributions are typically used to purchase an annuity. *Compare* **defined benefit plan** (*see* **defined benefit formula**), where the amount of the benefit is fixed in advance by a formula.

---

**delayed vesting:** *see* **vesting.**

---

**discounting of pension:** in some pension plans, an individual may retire prior to normal pensionable age and collect a pension that is reduced, or discounted, to reflect the additional number of years he or she will live to collect it, according to actuarial assumptions.

---

**early retirement:** retirement prior to normal pensionable age, usually with a discounted pension. Some plans, however, have early retirement provisions under which long-service employees may retire with a full pension. Corporations anxious to "downsize" may offer sweetened early retirement provisions, on a one-time-only basis. These still can be hard to swallow.

---

**employer-sponsored plan:** any pension plan offered by an employer. Usually a registered pension plan.

---

**equity fund:** *see* **Registered Retirement Savings Plan.**

---

**expectation of life:** actuaries' estimate of the number of years of life remaining to an individual who reaches a particular age, according to mortality tables. Where they sit, your days *are* numbered.

---

**fixed-income fund:** *see* **Registered Retirement Savings Plan.**

---

**full vesting:** *see* **vesting.**

---

**fully funded:** a pension plan judged by actuaries (there they go, making those assumptions again) to have sufficient assets to provide for the payment of all pension and other benefits that will have to be paid to both current and future pensioners. *See also* **funding.**

---

**funding:** the accumulation of assets from contributions and earnings to meet the future obligations (also called liability) of a pension plan. A fully funded plan is one without unfunded liability. Where unfunded liability exists, the company is required to inject additional assets. Government plans, such as the CPP, are not required to fund their liabilities, since, as Judy LaMarsh pointed out in introducing the CPP, the government, unlike a corporation, cannot go broke. It can, however, get awfully close.

---

**fund performance ratings:** assessment of the performance of a pension fund over a specified period of time. Useful reading in picking an RRSP equity or income fund, and much like studying the racing form: you look for signs of a winner.

---

**GIC plan:** *see* **Registered Retirement Savings Plan.**

---

**Guaranteed Income Supplement (GIS):** supplement to Old Age Security available to people with low incomes. The one pension you hope you won't collect.

---

**indexed pension:** a pension plan where payments are regularly and automatically increased in line with the rate of inflation. A controversial feature of some public-sector pension plans, including those for members of parliament and government ministers, and for the federal civil service. Abhorred in a certain quarter of the private sector, and especially by the National Citizens' Coalition. *Compare* **ad hoc adjustment.**

---

**insured pension plan:** plan in which contributions are paid directly to an insurance company for the purchase of annuities.

---

**integration with CPP/QPP:** a common practice in many private-sector pension plans, involving the reduction of the employee's pension by a portion of the amount due to that employee in CPP/QPP, to reflect contributions by the employer to the public plan on the employee's behalf.

---

**locking in:** requirement under federal or provincial legislation that pension contributions made by the employee and those made on his or her behalf by the employer must remain within the plan once the employee reaches a certain age or fulfills a certain number of years of service or plan membership. After that date, contributions can be neither forfeited by nor returned to the employee if he or she is terminated, and a deferred pension must eventually be paid instead. *See also* **return of contributions, vesting.**

---

**mandatory retirement:** when employers require that employees automatically retire on reaching a certain age, usually sixty-five. Such requirements face legal attack under the Canadian Charter of Rights, and appear unlikely to survive (which is how many employers view the prospects of a staff older than sixty-five).

---

**money purchase plan:** the most popular form of defined contribution plan.

---

**noncontributory pension plan:** a pension plan requiring no contributions from the employee.

---

**normal pensionable age:** the earliest age at which a member of a pension plan can retire on a full pension. *See also* **discounting of pension.**

---

**normal retirement age:** the age at which employees normally retire from the service of an employer. Typically sixty-five, but *see* **mandatory retirement.**

---

**Old Age Security** (OAS): noncontributory federal pension plan, with benefits starting at age sixty-five. Payable in full to all Canadians who have lived in Canada for a total of forty years after reaching the age of eighteen. For those who must survive on a public pension plan, old-age "security" is something of a misnomer.

---

**partial vesting:**   *see* **vesting.**

---

**past service:**   service by an employee that is recognized for the purpose of a pension plan, even though the service was performed before the employee became a member of that plan. In a contributory plan, retroactive contributions may be required on the part of the employee to have past service included in the benefit formula. Past-service liability is the liability assumed by an employer for benefits in respect of service performed by employees before the introduction or amendment of a pension plan.

---

**pay as you go:**   plan in which pensions are paid from current revenues, or other sources external to the plan, with no assets set aside to fund future obligations. (*See* **funding**.) Only the government can get away with this.

---

**pension:**   regular payments made to a retired employee under the terms of a pension plan.

---

**pension fund:**   the fund into which contributions are paid, for investment by a professional fund manager.

---

**pension income deduction:**   the first $1,000 of pension income is deductible for tax purposes. This provision applies from age sixty on to income from a pension fund (unless it is income from a survivor or disability pension, which is eligible at any age), and from age sixty-five on to income from private sources, such as an individually purchased annuity or RRSP.

---

**portable pension:** arrangement permitting an employee who leaves the service of one employer to transfer accumulated pension credits to the pension fund of a new employer. Desirable for the highly mobile individual who changes jobs frequently, leaving behind a string of minuscule deferred pensions or qualifying only for return of contributions, and thus earning only a minimal pension on retirement. A good idea—at least for the employee—that is rarely practiced, and then more often in public-sector than private-sector plans. Improved portability is the door to a better retirement and one of the main issues in discussion of pension reform.

---

**profit-sharing pension plan:** a pension plan of the defined contribution variety, where the employer's contributions fluctuate with profits. If the plan is a Registered Pension Plan under the Income Tax Act, the employer must contribute a minimum of one percent of the employee's remuneration annually. Unlike an ordinary employee profit-sharing plan (*see* p. 135), the employee pays no tax on his or her share of the profits until pension payments begin. The plebs' version of the typically more lush deferred profit-sharing plan (*see* p. 132).

---

**public pension plan:** a pension plan provided by the government, such as Old Age Security or CPP/QPP. Pension plans offered by the government in its role as an employer, such as civil-service and teachers' pension plans, are *not* described as public pension plans but as public sector plans.

---

**QPP:**   *see* **CPP.**

---

**refund right:**   *see* **return of contributions.**

---

**Registered Pension Plan (RPP):**   An employer-sponsored pension plan that meets the requirements of federal and provincial governments for registration under the Income Tax Act, and thus qualifying for favorable tax treatment.

---

**Registered Retirement Income Fund (RRIF):** plan that allows continued investment of funds withdrawn from an RRSP to avoid paying tax on them. By rolling over all or part of your RRSP into an RRIF, you can carry on the deferral of tax on your capital and on earnings within the plan, allowing your money to continue to grow. The plan provides a flexible scale—subject to a minimum—of increasing payments until you reach age ninety, with the amounts in a growing proportion of the whole determined by a formula based on your current age. You may withdraw additional sums, which are taxable. As with an RRSP, you can opt for a self-directed plan, or have the funds invested for you in GICs or an equity fund or fixed-income fund (*see* **Registered Retirement Savings Plan**). An RRIF is particularly appropriate if you do not need large payments in the early years of retirement. Otherwise, you may prefer to purchase an annuity, or to opt for combinations of the two. (You can have more than one RRIF or annuity.) If you think reading about RRIFs is rough, wait'll you get to RRSPs.

---

## Registered Retirement Income Plan (RRIP):
Not to be confused with R.I.P., though both offer peace of mind. General term for the various retirement income plans registered under the Income Tax Act, including registered pension plans and deferred profit sharing plans.

---

## Registered Retirement Savings Plan (RRSP): a
savings plan for retirement approved under the Income Tax Act, under which taxes are deferred on both the contributions and the income they earn until funds are withdrawn. Annual contributions are subject to contribution limits. There are various types of RRSPs, including:

*savings-account plan: offered by banks, trust companies, insurance firms and credit unions, these plans pay regular savings-account interest. They carry no administration fees and are highly liquid. However, they offer what are typically the lowest yields of any RRSP (unless you have bad luck with your RRSP equity fund).

*GIC plan: invests your money in a fixed-term guaranteed investment certificate (GIC), typically paying a higher guaranteed rate of interest than an RRSP savings account. Terms can vary from a month to ten years. Also called a fixed-term plan.

*fixed-income fund: does not offer a fixed rate of return, despite the name. Instead, it is a fund in which the assets are invested in one or more instruments yielding a fixed rate of return, such as preferred shares, bonds, mortgages and Treasury bills. Considered a more conservative investment than an RRSP equity fund because of its stability. If interest rates drop, you're safe. But if they rise, you may be safe *and* sorry.

**\*equity fund:** a mutual fund invested in the stock market, available through banks, trust companies, insurance firms, brokers and fund dealers. Equity funds offer a higher potential for growth in capital than other RRSP vehicles, but because they are tied to the stock market, they can also show a negative return. Some equity funds are invested in a relatively conservative way, while others pursue a more aggressive, high-growth strategy. It's up to the investor to determine the degree of risk he or she is prepared to incur. Remember, too, that a fund is only as good as its fund manager. Check the long-term performance ratings published in the financial press. Sales commissions, which are typically front-loaded—payable at the start—are also listed in the press.

**\*self-directed** RRSP: an RRSP in which you make the investment decisions. Available through some banks, trust companies and brokerage houses for a relatively low administration fee; you must also pay trustee fees and sales commissions on your transactions. Recommended only for sophisticated investors, or for those who already have other nest eggs in other baskets.

---

**Registered Retirement Savings Plan withdrawal options:** all RRSP holdings must be withdrawn by the end of the year in which you reach age seventy-one, or they become fully taxable. The main withdrawal options include cash (the least attractive, since it erases all or a large part of the tax benefits), annuities and Registered Retirement Income Funds.

---

**retirement age:**   *see* **normal retirement age.**

---

**return of contributions:**   when an employee's employment is terminated, the employee may be entitled to make a cash withdrawal of his or her own contributions (but not the employer's contributions on the employee's behalf) to a contributory pension plan. Such a withdrawal is possible only prior to vesting of the contributions. Once vesting has taken place, the employee's contributions remain in the pension fund until the payment of a deferred pension at the normal pensionable age. *See* **locking in, vesting.**

---

**rollover:**   the transfer of property from one form of investment to another without triggering tax at the time of transfer. For example, transfer of funds from an RRSP to a Registered Retirement Income Fund or of registered pension monies to an RRSP. Try not to rollover, then play dead.

---

**RRSP:**   *see* **Registered Retirement Savings Plan.**

---

**spousal RRSP:**   an RRSP where one spouse makes the contributions to—and claims the tax deduction for—a plan in the name of the other spouse.

---

**survivor benefits:** continued benefits paid by some pension plans to a designated beneficiary (*see* p. 180) in the event of the death of the plan member.

---

**unit benefit formula:** type of defined benefit formula that provides a unit of pension equal to a percentage of an employee's earnings for each year of membership in the plan. For example, a career-average or final-average benefit formula. *See* **benefit formula.**

---

**universal pension:** a public pension plan for the entire population. Old Age Security is a universal pension plan (subject to residence requirements), while CPP/QPP is only for members of the work force.

---

**vesting:** the process through which, at a particular point in time, an employee becomes entitled to the employer's contributions made on his or her behalf to a pension plan. Prior to vesting, an employee who is terminated may be entitled to make a cash withdrawal of his or her own contributions (*see* **return of contributions**) but has no legal claim on the employer's contributions. Once vesting occurs, both the employee's and employer's contributions are locked in, even if the employee is subsequently terminated. If termination occurs prior to retirement, the employee will then be entitled to a deferred pension.

Most pension plans operate on a basis of delayed vesting, so that the employee does not have a claim on the employer's contributions until he or she reaches a certain age or number of years of service, or both. Pension plans under federal jurisdiction have required that full vesting take place for employees who have attained age forty-five with ten years of participation, and most provincial statutes make the same requirement.

However, a recent federal reform (also in effect in some provinces) stipulates that vesting take place for employees after two years of plan membership. This involves contributions made after the qualification date. For those made before, the previous legislation still holds. The rest of the provinces are expected to follow suit eventually.

Some pension plans already make more generous provisions, such as earlier vesting. Where full vesting takes place after five years, for example, an employee terminated after more than five years but less than ten can choose between a return of contributions and a deferred pension. Other plans provide for immediate vesting of the employer's contributions, either in full or in part, making the employee immediately entitled to either a full or partial benefit. Under graded vesting, there is a gradual progression from no vesting through partial vesting to full vesting of the employer's contributions.

Although vesting is intended to protect the interests of the employee, it can be a two-edged sword for those who change jobs frequently. Increasing job mobility is therefore paving the way to a greater acceptance of portable pensions. That way, you *can* take it with you.

---

CHAPTER NINE

# *Family Finances and Estate Planning*

**administrator:** individual or trust company appointed by the court to administer the estate of a person who has died intestate. A female administrator is called an administratrix.

---

**age-forty trust:** trust held for the benefit of a single individual, to be payable not later than age forty. A common tax-planning device for wealthy individuals in the period when the federal government and most provinces charged a gift tax, since gifts could be made to such a trust without attracting tax.

---

**age of majority:** the age at which an individual can legally act on his or her own behalf; it's eighteen in Canada. (Age of reason is another matter; for some of us it never arrives.)

---

**alimony:** allowance made to a former spouse for his or her support after a divorce. (For tax implications, *see* p. 125.) Not to be confused with acrimony, although the two often go hand in hand.

---

**authentic will:** form of will, peculiar to the province of Quebec although recognized in other jurisdictions, executed before two notaries or before one notary and two witnesses. Also called a notarial will.

---

**beneficiary:** individual designated to receive all or part of the benefits of a will, trust or deferred-income plan. In estate planning, it is important to name a specific beneficiary for the proceeds of pension plans, deferred profit-sharing plans and RRSPs, or these proceeds will be taxed as a lump sum following your death. If you name your spouse as beneficiary, he or she can defer taxes by rolling over the proceeds into an RRSP. If you don't name your spouse as beneficiary, just remember: Hell hath no fury like a partner spurned.

**bequest:** a disposition of personal property in a will. *See also* **devise, legacy.**

**buy-sell agreement:** contract between two or more parties, such as partners in a business relationship, stating the procedures for one party to buy out the interests of the other. Without such an agreement, conflict may result when one partner dies and his or her spouse or children take over the deceased's share of the business. Often accompanied by a form of crisscross insurance (*see* p. 60), in which each insures the other to provide the necessary cash for the buy out.

**buy-sell insurance:** an insurance policy taken out to fund a buy-sell agreement.

**capital cost allowance:** a deduction against income to cover depreciation in the value of an asset. When a taxpayer gives away an asset, he or she is regarded as having made a deemed disposition of it at its fair market value. In estate planning, if the depreciable property is left under a will, it is deemed to have been transferred at the midpoint between its undepreciated capital cost—which is the original cost minus all deductions with regard to capital cost allowance—and its fair market value. If this deemed value exceeds its undepreciated capital cost, tax will be payable on the difference as recaptured capital cost allowance. These rules, however, do not apply to gifts between spouses during their lifetimes, to bequests to a spouse or to gifts to a spouse trust. Where the asset passes to the spouse, tax will not become payable on the recaptured capital cost allowance until the spouse disposes of the asset or dies. Where an asset on which depreciation has been taken is being left to a person other than the spouse, you can't just give and forget: provision should be made, in estate planning, for sufficient cash to take care of income tax payable on recaptured capital cost allowance, as well as on taxable capital gains. Otherwise, the recipient may be forced to sell the asset to pay the tax bill—and he sure won't remember you in his prayers. (*See also* **capital cost allowance,** pp. 128–129.)

---

**capital gain:**   the profit on the sale of an asset for more than its purchase price, taxable at one-half the normal tax rate. All property and assets on which a capital gain has accrued, with the exception of a principal residence, are subject to tax on capital gain in the event of the owner's death. This tax is payable by the individual's estate. As with tax on recaptured capital cost allowance, it can, however, be deferred if the property is left to the spouse. Tax is then not payable until the spouse disposes of the property, or dies. Since the capital gain may well have increased by this point, your heirs could face a huge tax bill. Provision can be made to pay this tax by the purchase of an insurance policy, payable on your death to your heirs. It is also possible for a spouse to elect to pay capital gains tax on receiving the property, a strategy that may make sense if the assets are expected to grow rapidly. The recent introduction of tax-free capital gains up to a certain statutory limit has made this issue somewhat less pressing in estate-planning terms. (*See also* **capital gains tax,** p. 129.)

---

**child-care deduction:** expenses for child care deductible from employment income for tax purposes, to a current annual maximum of $2,000 per child younger than fourteen and an overall maximum of $8,000. Try to find a day-care center or baby-sitter for that kind of money.

---

**codicil:** an instrument in writing, executed by the testator, that adds to, alters, explains or confirms the details of a previously made will, and brings the date of the will forward to the date of the codicil. Handy if you have second thoughts about your third cousin.

---

**co-executor:** where more than one executor is named in a will, each is known as a co-executor.

---

**common-law marriage:** relationship in which a couple live together as though they were married, without going through a legal marriage ceremony. Note, however, that to qualify for common-law status, the couple must present themselves to the community as being married—just living together doesn't count (so your mother isn't the only one who thinks that). Common-law spouses often have no status under intestacy laws—the legal spouse, if there is one, has the primary claim, although children born of the common-law relationship share equally with children born of a legal marriage. To provide for a common-law spouse (or for the significant other in any nonmarital relationship, for that matter), it is preferable to have a will specifically naming that person as a beneficiary, or else to make provision for a common-law spouse by means of an inter-vivos trust.

---

**community of property:** this is going to be complicated. Community of property was the legal regime prevailing in the province of Quebec until 1970, under which the surviving spouse in a marriage was automatically considered to already own fifty percent of the couple's total assets (unless there was a marriage contract stating separate ownership of property). Community of property has been replaced, under Quebec law, by the somewhat similar regime of partnership of acquests. "Acquests" are all property held by the couple not declared to be private property, which neither spouse can give away without the other's consent. It is possible, and sometimes advisable, to opt out of this arrangement by drawing up a marriage contract. If you do live in Quebec, look into this carefully. In other provinces, despite legislative changes in recent years, separation of property rather than community of property remains the rule. *See also* **Family Law Act (Ontario).**

---

**co-ownership:** situation in which two or more people have an ownership interest in the same property.

---

**cost base:** the amount paid for a property, used in calculating capital gains.

---

**crisscross insurance:** form of life insurance in which two or more persons insure each others' lives, often used in conjunction with buy-sell agreements. Winner takes all. Also known as partnership insurance.

---

**death benefit:**   an amount payable on the death of an individual under an insurance policy or pension plan.

---

**death duties:**   taxes payable on death, also called succession duties or estate taxes. There are no longer any federal or provincial death duties in Canada. However, capital gains taxes (*see* p. 129) can have much the same impact without careful estate planning. You'll not go tax-free into that good night.

---

**deemed disposition:**   under certain circumstances, a property is deemed to have been disposed of under the Income Tax Act, even though the property has not in fact been sold. As a result, there is a deemed realization of capital gains or losses, and taxes may be payable. Situations of deemed disposition occur when property is given away, when a person becomes a nonresident of Canada or when he or she dies, unless the property passes to the spouse or to a spouse trust. So it seems you're deemed if you do and deemed if you don't. (*See also* **capital cost allowance, capital gain.**)

---

**designated beneficiary:**   individual designated to receive the proceeds of a life-insurance policy or annuity.

---

**devise:**   legalese for a disposition of real estate in a will. Technically distinct from all non-real-estate gifts in a will, which are known as legacies. For beneficiaries in need of a place to live, a real-estate bequest is a blessing in devise.

---

**disinherit:** to deliberately exclude a spouse or child from a share in your estate under the terms of a will. Such a provision is usually ineffective in respect of a spouse or dependent child because of provincial laws requiring support. Nevertheless, a useful threat for keeping the family in line.

---

**disposition:** any transfer of an asset, either an actual disposition via gift or sale or a deemed disposition in the event of a death. If you're the recipient, should improve *your* disposition.

---

**distribution:** the division of an individual's assets under the terms of his or her will, supervised by the executor.

---

**endowment insurance:** cash-value life insurance payable either on reaching a specified age or else to a designated beneficiary in the event of death. (*See also* p. 63.)

---

**equivalent-to-married exemption:** provision of the Income Tax Act allowing a single parent to claim the same exemption for one child as could be claimed for a dependent spouse.

---

**escrow:** money or documents placed in trust with a third party.

---

**estate:** all money and property owned by a deceased individual. Too bad . . . you can't take it with you.

---

**estate freeze:**   tax-planning device, often involving a holding company (*see* p. 106), to reduce the capital gains tax bite in the event of your death. The basic principle is to freeze the value of your assets by shifting all future growth in them to your children and leaving the taxman out in the cold.

---

**estate planning:**   the process of arranging your financial affairs to ensure that your money and property go where you want them to after your death, with a maximum payout to your heirs and a minimum yield to Revenue Canada. Dividing well is the best revenge.

---

**estate splitting:**   structuring a will to ensure maximum use of tax savings and deferrals by directing all assets that would not otherwise be tax exempt to the spouse, and assets that are tax exempt (for example, a principal residence) to other beneficiaries. Never look a gift house in the mouth.

---

**estate taxes:**   *see* **death duties.**

---

**executor:**   individual or company named in a will to manage the estate according to the wishes of the deceased. A female executor is called an executrix.

---

**Family Law Act (Ontario):**   1986 law establishing a new regime for partners within a marriage or quasimarital relationship. The act recognizes marriage as a form of partnership, with property rights based on the equal position of the spouses as individuals, and provides for an equal division of property in the case of death or marital breakdown. So, when love and marriage no longer go together, one of you gets the horse and the other gets the carriage.

---

**fiduciary duty:**   the legal obligations of a trustee to deal fairly with the trust property; the trustee can't use it for his or her own enrichment.

---

**generation skipping:**   leaving property to your grandchildren rather than your children. This is one way of widening the generation gap.

---

**gift:**   transfer of money or property without recompense. People with large estates often try to limit their growth by gifting of assets to children or to a trust, to avoid payment of capital gains tax after they die. However, such a transfer, unless structured carefully, can still trigger income tax, capital gains tax or recapture of depreciation (*see* **capital cost allowance,** pp. 128–129). See **income attribution rules.**

---

**gift tax:**   direct tax on the donor of property the value of which exceeds a maximum allowable amount. No gift taxes are currently in effect in Canada, although Revenue Canada may give it to you in other ways. *See* **income attribution rules.**

---

**guardian:**   individual designated in a will, or else by the court, to be responsible for the physical care of children or others unable to look after themselves.

---

**holograph will:**   despite the name, a very low-tech proposition. An entirely handwritten will, signed by the testator, which is valid even without witnesses if recognized under the laws of the jurisdiction within which it was signed.

**inadequate consideration:** the transfer of assets for an amount less than their fair market value. (Also, how your heirs may feel about your will.)

**income attribution rules:** tax rules limiting the ability of a high-income earner to shift income, via income splitting, to a spouse or child who has a lower tax rate. For example, if you transfer money or ownership of an income-producing asset, such as stocks or bonds, to a spouse or child under age eighteen, the income produced by this gift must be reported with your investment income and you pay tax on it. Sorry: the buck stops here.

**income splitting:** transferring property to your spouse or children to reduce or eliminate tax on the income it earns. Useful where other family members are not taking full advantage of their $1,000 deduction on investment income (perhaps because they are still in diapers), or where they will pay tax on the income at a lower marginal rate than you would. Note, however, that you may fall afoul of the income attribution rules.

**in loco parentis:** in the place of the parent. How a guardian acts. Loco is how a guardian sometimes feels.

**inter-vivos gift:** a gift made between living persons, as opposed to a bequest made in a will.

**inter-vivos trust:** a trust established by a living person, as opposed to a testamentary trust, which is set up through the provisions of a will.

---

**intestacy laws:** provincial laws specifying the way in which an estate will be divided when an individual dies intestate.

---

**intestate:** a person who dies without leaving a will is said to die intestate. If you die intestate, your assets are typically frozen while the court appoints someone to wind up the estate. The estate is then distributed according to the provisions of the relevant provincial intestacy laws, which may or may not be in line with your own wishes, or with your family's particular needs. Intestate is no state to be in.

---

**last will:** the last will and testament is the one that is binding. Every new will is your last will, and formally revokes all previous wills until the next one—although it's also possible to update an existing will through the addition of a codicil. Your will should be reviewed periodically to reflect changing family needs and circumstances. But you can't appease everybody. (Nor can everybody have appease of the pie.)

---

**legacy:** a gift in a will (other than a gift of real estate, which is technically known as a devise). A universal legacy leaves the estate as a whole to one or more persons. A general legacy divides up the estate in fractions, which will go to a number of people. A particular legacy specifies an actual sum of money, or particular asset, to go to a particular individual. Particular legacies, much like preferred shares, are the first charges on an estate, and must be paid off before any other distribution is made.

---

**listed personal property:** under the Income Tax Act, a special category of personal-use property that specifies items, such as coins, stamps, rare books, art and jewelry, that frequently produce capital gains or losses (*see* p. 129) on their disposition. The gains are taxable, the losses are deductible against gains from similar property.

---

**marriage contract:** contract drawn up to provide for separate ownership of property. Common in the province of Quebec, where historically a community of property has otherwise applied, it is becoming more popular in other provinces: for example Ontario, where partners in a marriage may enter into a contract differing in terms from the Family Law Act, but may not overrule certain rights to the family home and obligations to children. Yes, Virginia, there is a Santa clause. *See* **Family Law Act (Ontario).**

---

**personal-use property:** assets used primarily for the personal use and enjoyment of the deceased individual (that's when he or she was alive; you *really* can't take it with you). Personal-use property, excluding that which qualifies as listed personal property, includes such items as cars, couches and lawn mowers. Since these are assets that depreciate greatly, Revenue Canada, in self-protection, has decreed any losses as nondeductible. However, in the rare event that someone should covet your sofa with the busted springs and popped buttons and will pay top dollar for it, the capital gains are taxable.

---

**preferred beneficiary election:** under the Income Tax Act, certain categories of beneficiaries of a trust can elect to pay tax on the trust income personally rather than through the trust. Makes sense where the personal tax rate is lower than that of the trust.

---

**probate:** literally, the process of proving before a court that a document is the genuine last will and testament of the deceased person. More commonly applied to the general process of executing a will. The stuff TV soaps are made of.

---

**Registered Educational Savings Plan (RESP):** method of saving for your child's post-secondary education. Unlike money you put into an RRSP (*see* pp. 167–168), contributions to a RESP are not tax deductible, but earnings within the plan are sheltered from tax until paid out to your child. Under many RESPs, your child must go to a post-secondary school and get past the first year to receive the full benefits. The tax is then payable by the child—a RESPonsibility you'll be happy to pass on.

---

**remarriage clause:** clause in a will to wind up a trust paying income to a spouse in the event of his or her remarriage, typically redirecting income to the children. No more Mr./Mrs. Nice Guy.

---

**right of survivorship:** the right to succeed to the ownership or part ownership of property following the death of the owner or part owner.

---

**settlor:**   individual creating a trust.

---

**spouse trust:**   trust set up for the sole benefit of a spouse, with no one else entitled to the income or capital while the spouse is alive. The assets of the trust are under the administration of a trustee rather than the spouse.

---

**succession duties:**   *see* **death duties.**

---

**testamentary trust:**   a trust set up under the provisions of a will on behalf of a deceased settlor.

---

**testator:**   the author of a will. If you've nothing left to will, you're the author of your own misfortune.

---

**trust:**   a bequest placing legal control of property with a trustee, who handles it on behalf of the beneficiary.

---

**trustee:**   a person who administers assets held in trust for another person. A trustee may be either named in a trust document or a will or be appointed by the court, and may be either an individual or a trust company. *See also* **fiduciary duty.**

---

**trust company:**   financial institution offering trust services as well as other financial services. It may make sense to appoint a company, rather than an individual, as a trustee, where a trust must be administered for a lengthy period, since the company can provide greater continuity. It's a good idea, however, to make provision to transfer the trust to another trust company in case the performance of the first one should prove inadequate. In some cases, a trust company may act as an agent appointed by the trustees to carry out the trust provisions of a will.

---

**trust officer:** individual working in the trust and estate-planning functions of a trust company.

---

**will:** the legally enforceable declaration of an individual's wishes for the distribution of his or her estate after death. Everyone has the right to make a will who meets provincial age requirements (typically age eighteen), is of "sound mind" and otherwise has the capacity to make a will. (When the flesh is willing, make sure the spirits are weak.) In Canada, different jurisdictions recognize different types of wills, including holograph wills, authentic wills (Quebec only) and the most common (and universally recognized) form deriving from the laws of England.

---

assigned risk,   80
assignment,   58
assumption of mortgage,   12
ATM (automated-teller machine),
    35, 45
attractive nuisance,   80
attribution rules, *see* income
    attribution rules.
audit,   126–127
authentic will,   175
authoritarian approach to
    investment,   96
automatic-premium loan,   58
automobile insurance,   80
average down,   96
average risk,   80
average up,   96
averaging,   127


balance due (taxes),   127
balance due on closing,   12
balance sheet,   3
balloon payment,   12
bank,   35
Bank Act,   35
bank card,   35
bank draft,   36
bankers' acceptances,   110
bank failure,   36
bank money order,   36
bankruptcy,   3
bank statement,   36
barter,   127–128
basis point,   97
bear,   97
bear market,   97
beneficiary,   58, 175–176
    contingent,   59, 71
    irrevocable,   66
    primary,   71
benefit, insurance,   58

benefit, pension,   157
benefit formula for pension,
    157–158
benefit period for insurance,
    59
benefits, *see* employee
    benefits.
bequest,   176, 177
best-average benefit formula,
    158
beta factor,   97
bid/ask price,   97
Big Board,   97
binder,   81
Black Tuesday,   98
blanket insurance,   81
blended payments,   12
blended rate,   13
block,   98
blue chip,   98
board lot,   98, 111
bond,   98, 116
bond discount,   98
bond premium,   98
bond rating,   98
bond value,   112
bond yield,   120–121
book value,   99
bridging loan,   13
broker:
    insurance,   81
    mortgage,   24
    stock,   99, 101
budget,   3
budgeting,   3
bull,   99
bull market,   99
business losses,   128
buying down,   13
buy order,   99
buy-sell agreement,   176
buy-sell insurance,   176

# Index

above par, 95
accelerated option, 57
accidental death benefit, 57
accident and sickness insurance, 57
accrual, 125
accrual rules, 125
acquests, 179
across the board, 95
act of God, 79
actual cash value, 79
actual damage, 79
actuarial assumptions, 157
actuary, 57, 157
additional insured, 79
ad hoc adjustment, 157
adjusted cost base, 134
adjuster, insurance, 79
administrator, administratrix, 175
advances versus declines, 95
adverse possession, 11
age-forty trust, 175
agent:
  insurance, 57
  real estate, 11
age of majority, 175
agreement of purchase and sale, 11
alimony, 125, 175
allowable business investment losses, 125
allowable capital losses, 125–126

American Stock Exchange (AMEX), 95
amortization, 11
amortization period, 11
amortization schedule, 11
ancillary benefits, 57
annual meeting, 95
annual renewable term, 57
annual report, 95
annuitant, 58
annuity, 58, 157
  deferred, 60, 159
  group, 64
  installment refund, 65
  joint and last survivor, 66
annuity certain, 58
annuity consideration, 58
antique, 4
appeal, on income-tax assessment, 126
apportionment, 79
appraised value of real estate, 11
appraiser, 11, 80
appreciation, 12, 126
arbitrage, 96
arm's length transaction, 96
assessed value, 12
assessment, income tax, 126.
  *See also* reassessment.
  municipal tax, 12
asset, 3, 35

call, 99, 112
Canada Deposit Insurance
    Corporation (CDIC), 36, 37
Canada Mortgage and Housing
    Corporation (CMHC), 13
Canada/Quebec Pension Plan
    (CPP/QPP), 128, 158
Canada Savings Bond (CSB),
    37, 125
Canadian Over-The-Counter
    Automated Trading
    System (COATS), 100
Canadian Real Estate Associa-
    tion (CREA), 13–14
capital, 3
capital cost allowance (CCA),
    128–129, 138, 143, 176–177
capital gain, 99, 125, 126, 129,
    177–178
    reserve in calculating, 148
capital gains, 134, 145, 186
    deemed realization of, 132,
    180
    on gifts, 177
capital gains exemption,
    129, 177–178
capital gains tax, 27, 129, 177,
    180
capital loss, 99, 129–130
    allowable, 125–126, 129–130
    deemed realization of, 132,
    180
capital markets, 100
career-average benefit formula,
    158
carrying charges, 130
    on property, 14
cash budget, 3–4
cash flow, 4
cashier's check, 37
cashless society, 37
cash surrender value, 59

cash value, 59
cash-value life insurance, 59,
    71
cash withdrawal, see return of
    contributions.
casualty insurance, 81
catastrophe, 81–82
catastrophe reinsurance, 82
certificate of deposit, 37
certificate of insurance, 59
certified Canadian feature
    film, 142–143
certified check, 38
charge account, 38
charge card, 35, 38
charitable donation, 130
chartered bank, 38
Chartered Life Underwriter
    (CLU), 59
chartist, 118
chattel, 14, 38
chattel mortgage, 38
check, 38–39
checking account, 39, 50
checking/savings account,
    39
child-care deduction, 130, 178
child tax credit, 130
claim, 82
claimant, 82
clearing, 39
clear title, 30
closed mortgage, 14
closing, 14
closing costs, 15
closing date, 15
COATS (Canadian Over-The
    Counter Automated
    Trading System), 100
codicil, 178, 185
co-executor, 178
coincident indicators, 106

coinsurance, 82
collateral, 39
collateral mortgage, 15
collectible, 4
collision insurance, 83
combination insurance, 83, 85
commercial banking, 50
commercial paper, 110
commercial property, 15
commission, 15, 100, 130–131
    front-loaded, 168
common disaster, 59
common-law marriage, 178–179
common stock, 100
community of property, 179, 186
company car, 131
compounding interest, 15–16
compound interest, 39
conditional offer, 16
conditional receipt, 62
condominium, 16
conjugal rights, 83
construction lien, see lien.
consumer loan, 39
Consumer Price Index (CPI), 4
contingent beneficiary, 59, 71
contribution limits, respecting
    RRSPs, 158–159, 167
contributory negligence, 79, 83
contributory pension plan, 159
conventional mortgage, 16
convertible bond, 100
convertible policy, 60
convertible preferred stock, 100
conveyance, 17
cooperative, 17
co-ownership, 179
correspondent bank, 40
co-sign, 40, 44
cost base, 179
counter check, 40
coupon, 100

coverage, 60
CPP/QPP, 128, 144, 158
credit bureau, 40
credit card, 40–41, 42
credit line, 46
creditor's group insurance,
    60
credit rating, 41
credit union, 41
crisscross insurance (partner-
    ship insurance), 60, 70,
    176, 179
cumulative preferred stock,
    101
current service, 159

daily-interest checking ac-
    count (DICA), 41
daily-interest savings account
    (DISA), 41
damages, 83
day order, 101
dealer (in securities), 101
death benefit, 159, 180
death duties, 180
debenture bond, 101
debit, 41
debit card, 42
debt, see liabilities.
debt load, 42
debt securities, 116. See also
    bond.
debt service, 42
decreasing term insurance,
    60
deductible clause, 83–84
deduction, 131
deed, 17
deemed disposition, 129,
    131–132, 137, 176, 180
deemed realization of capital
    gains or losses, 132, 180

default,   17
deferred annuity,   60, 159
deferred pension,   159
deferred profit-sharing plan (DPSP),
   132, 146
defined benefit formula,   159
defined benefit plan,   159
defined contribution plan,   160
deflation,   4
delayed vesting,   170–171
demand deposit,   42
demand loan,   42
dental expenses,   132
departure tax,   132
dependent,   132–133, 137
dependent child exemption,   133
depletion allowance,   133
deposit,   17
deposit insurance, see Canada
   Deposit Insurance Corporation.
depreciation,   128, 148. See also
   capital cost allowance.
depression,   101
designated beneficiary,   180
detached house,   17
devise,   180, 185
direct deposit,   42
disability,   60–61
disability allowance,   133–134
disability income insurance,
   60–61
disability waiver,   61
discharge,   17
discount brokerage,   101
discounting of pension,   160
discretionary account,   102
disinflation,   4
disinherit,   181
dismemberment benefit,   61
disposable income,   5
disposition,   134, 181
distribution,   181

dividend, life insurance,
   61, 69
dividend, on shares,   102
dividend income deduction,
   see investment income
   deduction.
dividend options,   61
dividend tax credit,   134
divorce,   134–135
dollar-cost averaging,   104
double indemnity,   57, 61–62
Dow Jones Averages,   102
down payment,   17
dread disease policy,   62
dues,   135
duplex,   18

earlier vesting,   171
early retirement,   160
earned premium,   62
earnings per share (EPS),   102
easement,   18
education allowance,   135
effective date,   62
effective interest rate,   18
electronic funds transfer (EFT),
   37, 42, 43
eligible (tax terminology),
   135
elimination period,   62
employee profit-sharing plan
   (EPSP), 135, 165
employee stock option
   benefits, 135–136
employer-sponsored plan,
   160
employment commission,
   see commission.
employment expense de-
   duction,   136
employment income,   136

endorse, 43
endorsement, 63, 84. *See also*
    rider.
endowment insurance, 63, 181
equity, 5
    in a property, 18
    shares in a corporation, 102,
    116
equity fund RRSP, 168
equity securities, 102, 116
equivalent-to-married exemption,
    133, 137, 181
escrow, 43, 181
escrow account, 17, 18
estate, 181
estate freeze, 182
estate planning, 182
estate splitting, 182
estate taxes, *see* death duties.
Eurobond, 102
Eurodollars, 102
evidence of insurability, 63
exchange rate, 103
exclusion, 84
exclusive listing, 18
ex-dividend, 103
executor, executrix, 182
exemptions, *see* personal
    exemptions.
expectation of life, 161
expense, 5, 137
    deductible, 131
expense allowances, 144
extended term insurance,
    63

face amount, 63
face value, 103
facility plan, 84
fair market price, 137
fall out of bed, 103
family allowance, 137

Family Law Act (Ontario),
    182–183
farm deduction, 138
federal dividend tax credit,
    *see* dividend tax credit.
federal foreign tax credit,
    138
federally registered com-
    pany, 63
Federal Reserve Board, 103
federal surtax, 138
federal tax, 138
fiduciary, 43
fiduciary duty, 183
final-average benefit formula,
    158
final-earnings benefit formula,
    158
financial planning, 3, 5
fire insurance, 84
first mortgage, 19
fiscal year, 103
fixed costs, 5–6
fixed-income fund RRSP,
    167–168
fixed-rate mortgage, 19
fixed-term RRSP, 167
fixtures, 19
flat benefit formula, 158
floater, 84
floating-rate mortgage, *see*
    variable-rate mortgage.
floor of stock exchange,
    104
floor trader, 104
flow-through shares, *see*
    tax shelter.
foreclosure, 19
foreign exchange, 43
formula investing, 104
forward averaging, *see*
    averaging.

four pillars of the financial-
    services industry,   43–44
friendly fire,   84–85
fringe benefits,   139
frontage,   19
front-end load,   104
front-loaded commissions,   168
frozen account,   44
full vesting,   170, 171
fully funded,   161
fund,   104. *See also* mutual fund.
fundamental analysis,   104
funding,   161
fund performance ratings,   161
fur floater, *see* floater.
futures,   105
futures exchange,   105
garnishment,   44
general legacy,   185
generation skipping,   183
gentrification,   19–20
GIC, *see* Guaranteed Investment
    Certificate.
gifts,   176–177, 183. *See also*
    bequest; devise; legacy.
  between spouses,   177
  inter-vivos,   184
gift tax,   175, 183
glamour stock,   105
gold certificate,   105
gold fix,   106
grace period,   64
graded vesting,   171
graduated life table,   64
gross debt service ratio (GDS),   20
gross income,   131, 139
gross-up,   134
group annuity,   64
group life insurance,   64
GTC (good till canceled),   111
Guaranteed Income Supple-
    ment (GIS),   144, 162

guaranteed insurability,   64
Guaranteed Investment
    Certificate (GIC),   44
  GIC RRSP,   167
guaranteed renewable
    insurance,   64, 69
guarantor,   44, 45
guardian,   183

handyman's special,   20
hazard,   85
hedge,   106. *See also*
    inflation hedge.
high-ratio mortgage,   20
holdback,   20
holding company,   106, 182
holograph will,   183–184
homeowner's policy,   20, 83,
    85
hostile fire,   84–85

immediate vesting,   171
inadequate consideration,
    184
income,   6
income attribution rules,
    139, 184
income property,   20–21
income splitting,   139, 184
income tax,   140
Income Tax Act,   140
incontestibility,   65
incorporation,   140
indemnify,   85
indexed pension,   162
Indexed Security Investment
    Plan (ISIP),   140
indicators, economic,   106
indirect tax,   140
individual life insurance,
    65
inflation,   4, 6

inflation hedge,   4, 6
inherent vice,   85
in loco parentis,   184
insider,   106
insider report,   106
insider trading,   106
insolvency, financial,   3
Inspector General of Banks,
     44–45
installment loan,   45
installment refund annuity,   65
insurability,   65
insurable interest,   85
insurable risk,   86
insurance,   65
insured,   65
insured pension plan,   162
integration with CPP/QPP,   162
Interac,   45
interest,   21, 107
interest adjustment date
     (IAD),   21
interest income deduction,
     *see* investment income
     deduction.
international money order,   36
inter-vivos gift,   184
inter-vivos trust,   179, 185
intestacy laws,   178, 185
intestate,   185
investment,   6
investment counselor,   6
investment income deduction,
     125, 129, 140
investment property,   20–21
investment tax credit,   140–141
investor,   107
IOU,   45
irrevocable beneficiary,   66
issue of securities,   107

jewelry floater, *see* floater.

joint account,   45
joint and last survivor annuity,
     66
joint and several responsi-
     bility,   40, 44, 45
joint insurance,   66
joint tenancy,   21, 29
junk bond,   107

key person insurance,   66
kiting,   46

lagging indicators,   106
land transfer tax,   21
lapsed policy,   66
last will,   185
leading indicators,   106
lease,   21
leasehold mortgage,   21
lease with option to purchase,
     22
leasing,   46
legacy,   180, 185–186
legal fees,   22
lessee,   22
lessor,   22
level premium insurance,   67
level term,   67
leverage,   22, 107, 109
liabilities,   3, 6
liability insurance,   22, 86
liability limits,   86
liability of a pension plan,
     161
libel insurance,   86
lien,   23
life annuity,   58
life insurance,   67
life underwriter,   57, 59
limited liability,   141
limited partnership,   107, 141
line of credit,   46

liquid assets, 108
listed personal property, 141, 186
listing, 23, 108
listing agent, 23
Lloyd's, 86–87
loading, 87
loan, 46
loan shark, 46
loan-to-value ratio, 23
loan value, 67
locking in, 162–163, 170
long-term investment, 108
loss, 87
lotteries, 141

maintenance, *see* alimony.
majority shareholder, 108
mandatory retirement, 163
"Manhattan duplex," 18
manipulation, 108
margin, 108–109
margin account, 107, 108–109
marginal rate, *see* rate of tax.
margin call, 109
market, 109
market average, 109
market price, 23, 109
market value:
    for real estate, 23
    for securities, 109
marriage contract, 186
    and partnership of acquests (Quebec), 179
married exemption, 133, 141–142
maturity, 67, 109
maturity date of mortgage, 23
maximum allowable deduction, 142

medical expenses deduction, 132, 142
merit rating, 87
MICR, 47
minority interest, 109
MLS, *see* multiple listing.
money market, 110
money-market instruments, 110
money order, 36
money purchase plan, 160, 163
money supply, 103, 110
Montreal Convention, 87
Moody's Investors Service 110
moral hazard, 85
morbidity rate, 68
mortality rate, 68
mortgage, 24
    closed, 14
    collateral, 15
    conventional, 16
    fixed-rate, 19
    high-ratio, 20
    leasehold, 21
    maturity date of, 23
    open, 26
    second, 24, 28
    term of, 30
    variable-rate, 16, 18, 31
    vendor-take-back, 24, 31
mortgage broker, 24
mortgage commitment, 24
mortgagee, 24
mortgage insurance, 24, 68
mortgage loan, 24
mortgagor, 25
motion picture tax shelter, 142–143
moving expenses, 143
MSE, 110

multibranch banking, 47
multiple listing, 18, 25
multiple-unit residential building
(MURB), 143
mutual fund, 110–111
mutual life-insurance company,
68

named perils, 87–88
net assets, see net worth.
net capital loss, 129–130
net income, 6, 131, 143
net worth, 3, 7
new money plan, 68
New York Stock Exchange (NYSE),
95, 102
no-fault insurance, 88
no-load fund, 104
nominal interest rate, 25
noncancelable policy, 69
non-capital loss, 143
noncontributory pension plan,
163
nonforfeiture options, 63, 69, 72
nonforfeiture value, 69
non-owned automobile policy,
88
nonparticipating policy, 69
nonsmoker plan, 69
nontaxable income, 141,
143–144, 146
nonvoting stock, 111
no-par-value stock, 112
normal pensionable age, 163
normal retirement age, 163
notarial will, 175
notice of assessment, 146–147
notice of loss, 88
notice of objection, 126
NSF, 47
numbered account, 47

NYSE, 111

OAS, 144, 163–164, 170
objection to income-tax
assessment, 126
odd lot, 111
odd-lot theory, 111
offer to purchase, 25
officer (corporate management), 111
Old Age Security (OAS),
144, 163–164, 170
open-ended investment
company, 110
open house, 25
open listing, 25
open mortgage, 26
open order, 111
opportunity cost, 7
option:
on a property, 26,
on stock, 99, 112,
114–115
ordinary life insurance, see
whole-life insurance.
overdraft, 46, 47
overdraft protection, 46, 47
overdrawn, 47
overimprove, 26
overinsurance, 88
over-the-counter securities,
101, 108, 112.
See also COATS.
owner of an insurance
policy, 70

package policy, see combination insurance.
paid-up insurance, 70
partial vesting, 171
participating policy, 61,
69, 70

participating policyholders, 68, 73
particular legacy, 185–186
partnership insurance (crisscross insurance), 60, 70, 176, 179
partnership of acquests, 179
party wall, 17, 28
par value, 95, 103, 112
passbook, 48
past service, 164
past-service liability, 164
pawnbroker, 48
pay-as-you-go plan, 158, 164
payee, 48
payor, 48
payroll deduction, 144
penny stock, 112–113
pension, 164
pension fund, 164
pension income, 144
pension income deduction, 128 144, 164–165
p/e ratio (price/earnings ratio), 113
peril, 88
"perks," 139
permanent disability, 70
permanent life insurance, 71
personal check, 48
personal exemptions, 132, 133, 144
Personal Identification Number, (PIN), 35, 48
personal income, 7
personal loan, 48
personal-use property, 145, 186
physical hazard, 85
PIT, 26
point of sale (POS), 48–49, 54
policy, 71
policy date, 71
policy dividend, 61

policyholder, 71
policy loan, 71
political contribution tax credit, 145
portable pensions, 165, 171
portfolio, 113
POS (point of sale), 48–49
possession, 26
postdated check, 49
power of sale, 26
preauthorized payment, 49
preferred beneficiary election, 187
preferred stock, 113
premium, 71, 113
prepayment clause, 27
price/earnings ratio (p/e ratio), 113
primary beneficiary, 71
primary coverage, 89
prime lending rate, 49
prime rate, 113
principal, 27, 114
principal residence, 27, 145
principal sum, 72
probate, 187
profit-sharing pension plan, 165
profit-sharing plan, 145–146
progressive income tax, 146
promissory note, 49, 146
proof of loss, 89
property tax, 27
property transfer on divorce, 134–135
pro rata, 114
prospectus, 114
provincial life-insurance company, 72
provincial tax, 146
proxy, 114

proxy fight, 114
Prudent Man Rule, 114
public pension plan, 165–166
public-sector plans, 165, 166
put, 99, 106, 112, 114


QPP, *see* CPP/QPP.
qualified property (for investment tax credit), 140–141
Quebec Pension Plan (QPP),
    *see* CPP/QPP.
quotation (quote), 115


random walk theory, 115
rate of insurance, 89
rate of tax, 146
raw material, 27
real property, 27
realtor, 27
reassessment, 146–147
recaptured capital cost allowance, 129, 176–177
recaptured depreciation, *see* capital cost allowance.
receiver, 3
recession, 101, 103, 115
reconciliation, 49
recovery, 115
red ink, 50
refinance, 27
refund, 147
refund right, *see* return of contributions.
Registered Educational Savings Plan (RESP), 187
registered encumbrance, 23, 27–28
Registered Home Ownership Savings Plan (RHOSP), 28, 147

Registered Pension Plan (RPP), 166
Registered Pension Plan deduction, 147
registered representative, 115
Registered Retirement Income Fund (RRIF), 166–167
Registered Retirement Income Plan (RRIP), 167
Registered Retirement Savings Plan (RRSP), 149, 167–168
    rollover into RRIF, 166
    types, 167–168
    withdrawal options, 168–169
reinstatement, 72
remarriage clause, 187
renewable term insurance, 57, 72
rental income, 148
rent insurance, 89
replacement cost, 28
replacement value, 89
rescission right, 72
reserve, 148
resident of Canada, ceasing to be, 132
retail banking, 50
retirement age, *see* normal retirement age.
retractable bond, 115
return of contributions, 169
Revenue Canada, 148
revolving credit, 46, 50
rider, 72. *See also* endorsement; waiver.
right of survivorship, 187
right of way, 28
risk, 89
rollover, 148, 152, 166, 169

row house, 17
RRSP, *see* Registered Retirement Savings Plan.
rule of 72, 115

safe-deposit box, 50
savings account, 50
savings-account RRSP, 167
Schedule A bank, 50–51
Schedule B bank, 50–51
schedule of insurance, 90
scientific research tax credit, 149
second mortgage, 24, 28
secured loan, 51
securities, 116
Securities Act, 116
security, 28
self-directed RRSP, 168
self-employed income, 136, 149
seller's market, 116
semidetached house, 17, 28
service charge, 51
settlement of insurance claim, 90
settlement options (life and health insurance), 73
settlor of trust, 188
shareholder, 116
shareholder's equity, 116
shareholder insurance, 73
share purchase tax credit, 149
short position, 116
short selling, 97, 116
short squeeze, 116
sign back, 29
simple interest, 51
single-premium whole life, 73
small investor, 116–117
SMART card, 51
sophisticated investor, 117
speculation, 117

speculator:
on real estate, 29
on securities, 107, 117
spousal RRSP, 169
spousal tax credit, *see* married exemption.
spousal transfers, 149–150
spouse trust, 177, 188
spread, 96
Standard and Poor's, 117
standard risk, 73
stand-by charge, automobile, 131, 150
standing order, *see* preauthorized payment.
statement of adjustments, 29
stock, 117
yield, 120
stock exchange, 117
stockholder, *see* shareholder.
stock life-insurance company, 73
stock market, 118
stock options deduction, *see* employee stock option benefits.
stop-loss order, 118
stop payment, 52
straight life insurance, 73, 75
stripped bond, 118
subrogation, 90
substandard risk, 73
succession duties, *see* death duties.
suicide clause, 74
sum insured, 63
superintendent of insurance, 74
surrendered policy, 74. See *also* cash surrender value; nonforfeiture options.

survivor benefits,   170
SWIFT,   52
syndicate, investment,   118

T1 General,   153
T1 Special,   153
T4 slip,   153
T5 slip,   153
take back, *see* vendor-take-back
   mortgage.
takeover,   118
taxable allowance,   150
taxable benefit, *see* fringe benefit.
taxable income,   150
taxation,   150
taxation year,   151
tax avoidance,   151
tax brackets,   146
tax credit,   151
tax deductible,   151
tax deferral,   152
tax evasion,   152
tax haven,   152
tax lien,   29, 152
tax planning,   151, 152
tax shelters,   129, 141, 145, 153
   motion picture tax shelter,
      142–143
tax shield,   153
T-bills,   53, 119
technical analysis,   118
tenancy in common,   29
tender offer,   118–119
term deposit,   44, 52
term insurance,   71, 74.
   *See also* convertible policy;
   renewable term
   insurance.
term of mortgage,   30
term to 100,   74
testamentary trust,
   185, 188

testator,   188
TFA1 slip,   153
third party,   90
third-party insurance,   90
three Cs of credit,   52
ticker tape,   119
time is of the essence clause,
   30
title,   30
title search,   30
total debt service ratio (TDS),
   30
townhouse,   30
trader,   119
transfer of property on
   divorce,   134–135
traveler's check,   52
Treasury bill,   53, 119
treasury stock,   119
trust,   53, 188
trust account, *see* escrow
   account.
trust company,   53, 188–189
trustee,   53, 188
   fiduciary duty of,   183
trustee in bankruptcy,   3, 53
trust officer,   53, 189
TSE,   119
TSE 300 Composite Index,
   119
tsunami damage,   90
tuition fees,   153

UIC,   154
UIC benefits repayment,   154
UIC benefits taxable,   154
unconditional offer,   16, 31
undepreciated capital cost,
   128–129, 176
underground economy,   154
underinsurance,   90
underinsured,   82

underwriter,   74–75
Underwriters' Laboratories,
    91
underwriting,   75, 120
unearned premium,   62
unfunded liability,   161
uninsured-motorist coverage,   91
unit benefit formula,   170
universal legacy,   185
universal pension,   170
unlisted stock, see over-the-
    counter securities.
valuation:
    appraisal of real estate,
        11
    of insured items,   80, 91
variable costs,   6, 7
variable interest rate,
    53–54
variable-rate mortgage,   16,
    18, 31
VCAN,   54
V-day,   154
vendor-take-back mortgage,
    24, 31
venture capital,   120
vesting,   169, 170–171
VSE,   120

waiver,   75. See also rider.

waiver of premium,   61
Wall Street,   120
war clause,   91
warrant,   120
Warsaw Convention,   87
"white painting,"   19–20
whole-life insurance,   75.
    See also endowment
    insurance;
    permanent life insurance.
will,   189
    authentic or notarial,
        175
    codicil to,   178, 185
    holograph,   183–184
    last,   185
withholding taxes,   144, 154
wraparound mortgage,   31

x,   120
xd,   120

year-end, see taxation year.
yield,   120–121

zero-coupon bond, see
    stripped bond.
zoning,   31–32